The People Smart Leader

Five Keys to Inspire Others to Do Their Best Work

Lindiwe Stovall Lester

Author of *The Everyday Leader*

The People Smart Leader, Five Keys to Inspire Others to Do Their Best Work

 First edition. 1st printing May 2024.

ISBN number: 978-1-7344826-7-6

Library of Congress Cataloguing-in-Publication Data

Lester, Lindiwe Stovall

The People Smart Leader, Five Keys to Inspire Others to Do Their Best Work

- Leading People
- Business Management
- Personal Development
- Team Development
- Workplace Culture
- Leadership Coaching
- Interpersonal Skills

For information or inquiries: info@pseinstitutebooks.com or www.pseinstitutebooks.com

Dedicated to yesterday's, today's, and tomorrow's leaders upon whom we count to light the way for a better world.

This is a tribute to my grandsons, Jide and Zaire—the future—and my late father, Willie Stovall Jr., who in his time, was a courageous, distinctive leader.

CONTENTS

This book encourages you to move from knowing what you should do to doing the work to evolve your real-world leader practices. Take the journey and watch yourself flourish as a *People Smart* leader.

Get Right to It: Most Crucial Considerations

What is it like to be led by you?

Do you ever ask yourself that question? Do people succeed and thrive with you as their leader?

This anonymous quote below voices the sentiment of many staffers; it indirectly shares the unpleasantness of having to report to or be led by a low skilled people leader:

> **5. "A bad job with a good boss is better than a good job with a bad boss." — *Unknown***

Such experiences are far too common, and that is why I authored another book on the *people aspects* of leadership. I want to support smart people, including you, in becoming exceptional at leading, inspiring, and evoking the best from their people.

This is a short opening section, a quick primer for you in the event you do not get through all Five Keys in this book. Use it to get started, and hopefully it will prompt you to delve deeper and work your way through the entire book. Mastering all five interrelated keys is essential for consistent, exceptional *people leadership.*

MAKE-OR-BREAK SKILLS FOR *PEOPLE SMART* LEADERS

The list below are habits, mindsets, and practices leaders, in their words, have shared with me as their obstacles, blind spots, self-identified growth areas, or requirements to advance their roles.

Can you relate to any of these?

- Balance empathy and getting results: how to have both.
- Get my team to be more cohesive and collaborative.
- Stop being so hands-on and find time to plan.
- Be better and more assertive during conflict.
- Improve how I work with different staff personalities.
- What to do about unmotivated staff.
- Manage my stress and set better boundaries.
- Less *firefighting* and more focus on meaningful work.
- Figure out the best use of my talents and strengths.
- How to be more inspirational for my people.
- Stop bossing, and coach people for growth.
- Provide feedback regularly in a way people can receive it.
- Every time I get a good hire, my team runs them away.
- I need to listen and think better.
- How to get my people to solve problems.
- How to stop staff complaints every time there is a change.
- End wasteful meetings that kill time and sap energy.
- I am loved, but my team isn't getting the work done.

Get ready to sharpen any of the above and other skills as you actively work through *The People Smart Leader*.

Do This First

Rate yourself on the *People Smart* Five Keys.

Before you dive into the chapters, rate yourself on some habits and skills that are important in leading others masterfully. Use this to highlight areas to prioritize for development, and to acknowledge the effective practices you already have in place.

Rating: 1-Never, 2-Rarely, 3-Sometimes, 4-Most times, 5, Always

		Rating
LEADING AND ALIGNING WITH THE MISSION		
1	I am clear about my organization's goals, and I lead and inspire my team members from that big picture view.	
2	Each direct report knows how their job is aligned with and helps the organization meet its goals.	
3	I interpret and manage organizational changes in a way that inspires my team to continue doing quality work.	
4	I am flexible, able to adapt my priorities as changes happen in my organization and among our customers.	
5	I practice self-awareness and address my mindset and energy to create an inspiring workplace for my team.	
CONNECTING & ENGAGING (RELATIONSHIPS)		
6	I communicate clearly and respectfully to all of my direct reports, listening intently and valuing their input.	
7	I model good, fair, and ethical management with my direct reports.	

8	I take time to build a relationship with each direct report, learning their strengths, stories, motivators, and growth needs.	
9	I work to remove any barriers that impede my team members' work success.	
10	I seek out and listen to team members thoughts and feedback on how I and the team can be more effective.	

COACHING AND FEEDBACK

11	I schedule time once or twice monthly to talk (and listen) to each person about their growth goals and challenges.	
12	I encourage team members to come up with solutions to their issues, rather than always telling them how to think and what to do.	
13	I consistently deliver both positive and challenging feedback to my direct reports to help them grow.	
14	I show courage (combined with caring) when providing corrective performance feedback.	
15	I focus more on making use of team members' strengths rather than drilling them about their weaknesses.	

ONGOING DEVELOPMENT

16	Each year, I think about my current skills, identify learning goals, and develop a plan so I keep growing.	
17	I pay attention to the quality of the team's culture and use strategies to maintain a healthy, collaborative work environment.	

18	I stay abreast of trends in our area of work through reading, workshops, or other means.	
19	I provide team members opportunities to gain experience and skills and to use more of their talents, via committees, new tasks, special projects, etc.	
20	I plan and lead meetings that: have a clear purpose, are organized and on time, and end with assigned follow-up.	

ACHIEVING TEAM PERFORMANCE

21	I meet with each team member to co-create their goals, hear their view of their performance, and how they'd like to grow.	
22	Each team member knows how well they are doing year-round, rather than just year-end.	
23	I regularly recognize the valuable work of each team member.	
24	I balance empathy with accountability for performance.	
25	My team is results-oriented, and we can be counted on to achieve our goals.	

Hindsight, Insight, Foresight

Looking back, what is one thing this activity makes clearer for me personally as a leader?

In which areas are you already very strong? *(e.g., those rated 4 or 5)*

As you move forward, which are your areas for attention?

When you've finished the book, come back and do this exercise again. Acknowledge your progress as a "People Smart" leader.

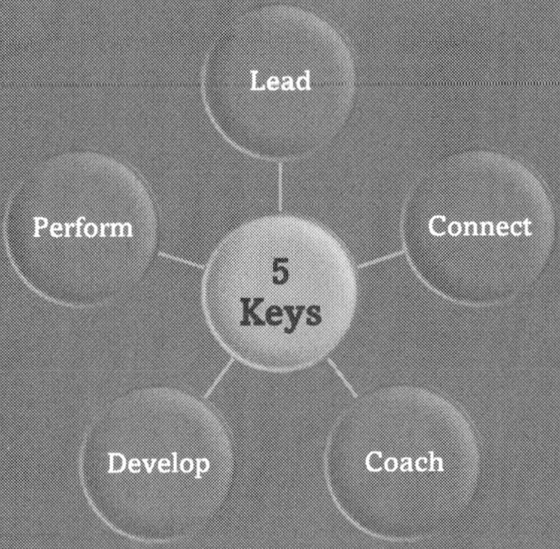

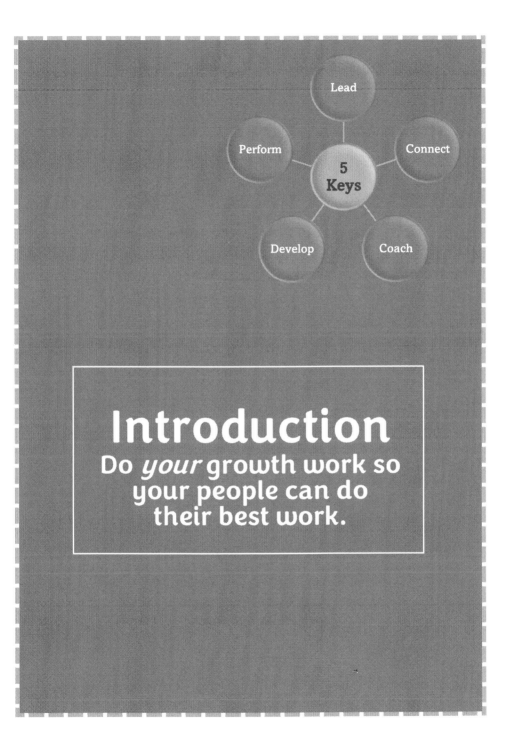

Introduction

Do *your* growth work so your people can do their best work.

Why should YOU consider leading with *People Smarts*?

I'll begin by sharing with you that I believed I was done writing for a while after my 2022 book, *The Everyday Leader*. Then, thanks to the open and sincere conversations with leaders and their teams, colleagues and mentees, this book emerged out of recurring themes, plentiful notetaking, new coaching client stories, and fresh research.

As an executive and leadership coach, I am privileged to work with some talented, high achieving people. Yet some have shown critical gaps in the "people smarts" domain that have undercut their brilliant strategies to greater or lesser degrees. I have partnered with leadership teams made up of incredibly talented individuals but whose collective results fall short of their potential. That has largely been due to their failure to work on how to synergize and maximize their members' skills. So here we are: *The People Smart Leader* book.

The ability to lead others adeptly is not a birthright. Leading people to do their best work is learned, and the learning doesn't stop. Anyone with people reporting to them should prioritize evolving and expanding their skills if they are to achieve stellar results.

Gallup's 2023 *State of the Workplace* study reiterated the supervising leader's critical role in the level of their team's engagement, which is key to staff delivering their best work. *"Engagement means your people are psychologically present to do their work. They understand what to do; they have what they need, and they have a supportive manager and a supportive team. They know why their work matters. They are ready."* (p. 9)

With the many changes in the workplace (many instigated by the Covid 19 pandemic), leading your staff effectively has become increasingly complex. That means elevating your leadership skills is necessary to position yourself for ongoing success into the future.

Many who have been selected to lead have had limited exposure to the "people" side of leadership skill-building. Relying on our technical smarts and previous experience, we, including me, have courageously jumped in, and followed where our wits led us. The effect of that strategy—we have likely experienced some successes alongside palpable exasperation and staff disaffection.

Admittedly some still follow the mantra of "fake it till you make it." Too often, we keep faking it until some of us come to believe our self-deception: "I'm pretty good at this." Such leaders can end up never forming and being guided by a values-based leadership philosophy to inform how you engage, make decisions, and shape your perspectives as you lead others. This has limitations.

Effective and admired leaders *do the work* to change and evolve how they lead. They go from bossing, micromanaging, and stressful interactions to inspiring, developing, and coaching for better results.

This book is here to nudge and support you as a "people" leadership practitioner, shifting from simply *knowing to doing* the actual transformational work of leading others well.

What is distinctive about *People Smart* leadership?

About seven years ago, 30 human resources professionals sought an answer to their most pressing query: *How can we guide our supervisors to be more effective leading their teams?* They requested an initial 45-minute *Lunch and Learn.*

To gain more clarity about how to support their request, I asked them what was *actually* happening. It boiled down to: *Managers are falling short of their team's goals, team members are unhappy, staff turnover is high, and managers are frustrated and stumped about what to do.* These HR directors' responses were unsurprising, consistent with management studies. I have paraphrased, in the table below, some of the mindset and skillset shifts they and other leaders were seeking.

From a culture of...	**To a culture of...**
Over-managing	Appropriate autonomy
Overworking	Delegating
Quick to fire	Good performance feedback, regular
Detachment	Connection
Aggression	Assertiveness
Telling	Asking and collaborating
Do as I say	Modeling quality
Task focus	Vision alignment
Blaming	Owning and self-development
"What's wrong" focus	Leveraging strengths & talents
Hours worked	Goal achievement
One size fits all	Individualized development
Single decision maker	More shared leadership, participatory
Command and control	Culture of creative problem solving
Primary role is boss	Primary function is developer, coach, supporter, and visioning

This is where this book began. With a 45-minute session, my colleague and I wanted to provide a set of actionable insights to support manager development and performance improvement efforts. We spent a few weeks fleshing out the persistent thematic *people leadership* gaps we saw among leaders at multiple levels. We also scoured the research to confirm and add to our themes. We wanted to help leaders begin to install the most productive and satisfying workplace for the team and themselves.

People Smart Five Keys

With the client's recommending that my team create something simple to understand, we distilled the ideas down to these five keys: LEAD, CONNECT, COACH, DEVELOP, and PERFORM.

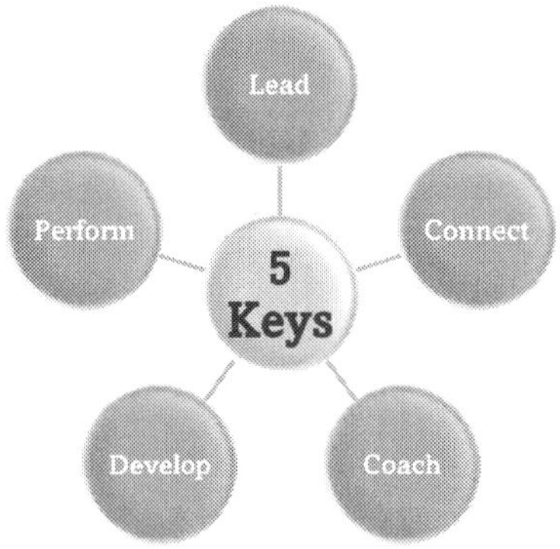

At the end of the *Lunch & Learn*, the directors said they gained lessons they could apply with the managers and to their own leadership around hiring, learning and development, and performance. They left upbeat, and with tactics for a way forward.

Since then, I continued building out each of the keys with concepts, real stories, exercises, and reflections that a leader can work through alone, with a coach, or in a peer learning circle. Thanks to my clients and colleagues, I've continued to assess and refine the strategies to ensure their durability in today's changing environment.

For example, real story, I suggested a new client read two chapters of my first book, *The Everyday Leader* (which introduced the Five Keys), that I thought related to her coaching goals. After reading and doing the included exercises, she said:

"I feel like I've grown exponentially just by reading the targeted chapters. I'm already rethinking some things. I feel ready to take on my new job, with different ways to approach the work and adapt my style to be effective." We both agreed to a shorter coaching schedule than we originally planned. That's a win!

As you work through the book, I hope you sense me supporting you, cheering for you, challenging you, and coaching you. Discover and engage more of your talents as you *put in the work* to lead others competently and confidently.

Is the book for you?

If you are a leader who is chief executive, C-suite, director, or coordinator, it's for you. Are you leading a governing board, a group of volunteers, or a committee? Ditto. If you are seeking to advance your career or learn how to be a stellar employee, you will find it useful. Are you a member of or heading a collaboration, cohort group, or coalition? *The People Smart Leader* will support you as well.

Why this book matters.

This book extends from *The Everyday Leader's* Section 3: Know and Grow Your People. It offers skill-building concepts not included in *The Everyday Leader* that support you in evolving your leadership. Some of the more crucial topics are presented again at a more detailed and experiential level.

Also, with no plans to expand my small coaching practice, I asked myself: *How can I be of greater value to those with The Everyday*

Leader or those who want more support working with their direct reports? This second book is my response.

I offer *The People Smart Leader* as an actionable, self-directed field guide for those in the growth zone. It can complement other efforts. In this book, I'm pushing harder for leaders to act, not just read.

Consistent quality leadership happens when there is both awareness AND commitment to evolve your leadership behaviors and mindset.

Gaps leaders identified.

Even those with MBAs might have people leadership skill gaps. Most business graduate programs focus on strategy, finance, global markets, human resources, supply chain and the like. Few build skills for leading individuals and teams.

The book is informed by recent input I received from 147 new and seasoned leaders (from 2020 to 2023). They believed tackling these skill gaps and upskilling themes would boost both their confidence and effectiveness. This book is intent on supporting them and you to leverage your current talents while also elevating your *people* skills.

How to use the book

The People Smart Leader is both distinct from and a complement to *The Everyday Leader*. There are five sections that line up with each of the FIVE KEYS with concepts, stories, reflections, and action steps.

I suggest you work through all five keys because they are interdependent, each one impacting the efficacy of the others. Maybe make a schedule to cover one key monthly or weekly. Then take breaks and apply the learning in real life. Breathe. Celebrate growth.

Implement a plan something like the process on the right.

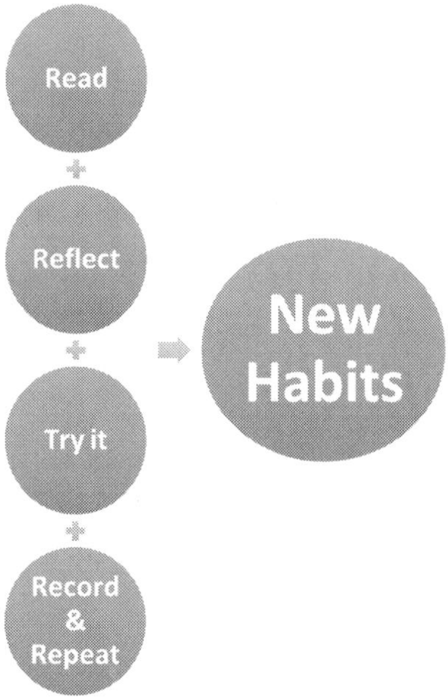

Read a work-related topic, **reflect** on the content, **try it** in your real work setting, **record** notes in the book, and **practice** until new habits actually stick, i.e., they are integrated and natural in your leadership practices.

You owe it to yourself and your team. People spend the largest part of their waking lives in a work setting. As such, every leader ought to be on an ongoing quest to develop their skills, refine and re-think their approaches.

Ready to refuel and conquer "staff issue" overload?

Is it time to proactively elevate your leadership to be ready for a next level move?

Is it time to shift from being instinctively good at leading others to acquiring exceptional, repeatable, and contemporary people leadership skills?

Want to become a leader who others admire and seek to emulate?

Then, get started.

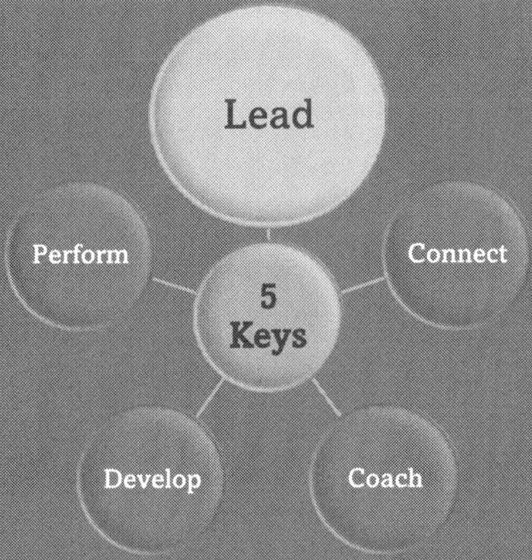

the LEAD key

The "People Smart" Leader is skilled leading their Unit, Themselves, and their People.

The LEAD Key: Triple lenses for leading people well

What are the main things we, as leaders, must know, believe, and do to lead others well?

Here's the first mental shift I believe is essential for leading others to deliver their best work: Begin seeing yourself as a leader rather than a boss-manager. *Manager*, a word commonly found in job descriptions and titles, could infer that people can be bossed into doing their work; that view has proven increasingly less reliable. You don't have to change your title, but changing your mindset is key. That involves facing the hard truth that "bossing" is a relic of the long-gone industrial age workplace.

Exploring the LEAD KEY will increase your people leadership efficacy. Think of **leadership** as *formal or informal positional authority; being responsible for engaging and developing the potential of others to achieve a goal; a role that influences others' ability to get things done.*

Three leadership lenses

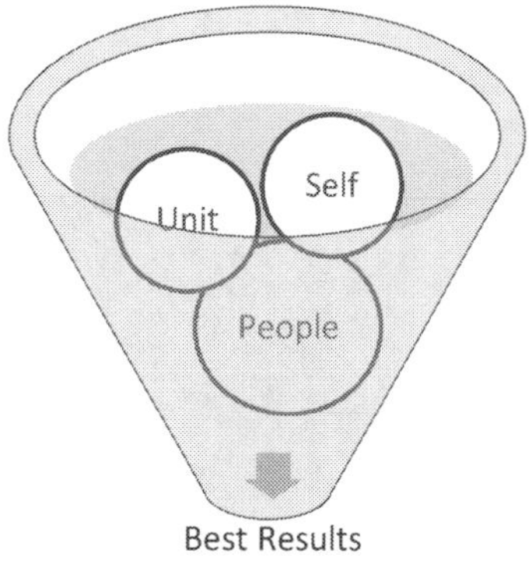

As a skilled "people" leader, examine your role from three interconnected vantage points: *Lead yourself, your unit, and your people.*

As you address all three, and maintain equilibrium with the three, you and your team can expect increased satisfaction, sense of purpose, and valued accomplishments.

Lead Yourself, Chapter 1

Though your main job is to lead the enterprise, this is a good place to start. Think: *A better you for better enterprise level performance.* Leading oneself is a frequently neglected area because most leaders' energy is directed outwardly—towards enterprise goals or their direct reports. Remember, the more attention invested in leading and growing yourself, the better the results will be for the other two areas. Use the concepts and exercises to better deploy your strengths, expose critical blind spots, and hone your leadership approach.

Lead Your Unit (or the Enterprise), Chapter 2

Depending on your job role, Leading the Unit means leading the entire enterprise, a department, or the area you are responsible for. Whatever the case, you will benefit from being highly adept at leading your unit. This chapter offers key concepts, reflections, and application activities for that.

Lead Your People, Chapter 3

The people who report to you are assets and are essential to achieving your organizational imperatives. You need them to be their best, feel their best, deliver their best, work together synergistically, and grow skills alongside you. How do you do that? By operationalizing all Five Keys in the book. The ideas and strategies in Chapter 3 (and later in Chapter 9) support you as you address the nuances and complexities of leading each person and the entire team.

✓Check-in: Which area should you spend more time on right now? Org____ Individuals_______ Team_______ Self-growth _______

Chapter 1

Lead YOURSELF

Some essentials that demonstrate evolved self-leadership:

1. Clarify your leadership approach, beliefs, and mindset.
2. Address your self-awareness gap.
3. Align your leadership presence: How are you showing up?
4. Mind your mood, energy state, and well-being practices.
5. Become a more agile thinker.
6. Improve receptivity to feedback and coaching.

The "Lead Yourself" topic makes up the longest chapter in this book (and may be worth expanding into its own publication). I believe it is a crucial component for becoming a long-term effective and admired leader. If that's something you strive for, attending to how you lead and manage yourself will prove to be a worthwhile investment. You can start by reflecting on your leadership thought processes, *how* you engage your talents, the beliefs and assumptions you hold, and the ways you are developing yourself. This is the focus of this chapter.

The greater your self-awareness, the greater chance you have of using your skills in the best way, adapting your habits as needed, and designing a plan to keep growing as a talented leader. Start by contemplating the questions on the next page.

Introspection Exercise

The following questions influence how you lead yourself and others, some of which you may not have thought about. For now, you will reflect and then mark those you want to explore later.

- ❍ Who am I as a leader?
- ❍ Why have I chosen to lead?
- ❍ What beliefs and personal values guide how I lead?
- ❍ What is the effect I want my leadership to have (on the organization and my team)?
- ❍ What exactly am I trying to accomplish as I work hard day after day? (my goal statement).
- ❍ What is it like for someone to be led by me?
- ❍ What are the unique strengths I bring to my role as a leader?
- ❍ What growth or learning do I need to pursue to be more successful for the organization and my team?
- ❍ What adaptations to my well-being practices do I need to make to be the best for myself and others?
- ❍ What impressions do I give about my leadership based on how I show up in meetings, with peers and my team?
- ❍ How might my mindset and fixed beliefs trap me in unproductive ways of engaging with people?
- ❍ Am I a leader who motivates people or depletes their energy?

Which 1-2 of these highly introspective questions would you like to have a clearer or more positive response to? Why? (Put your answers in the space provided on the next page.)

CLARIFY YOUR LEADERSHIP APPROACH AND MINDSET

What is the leadership philosophy (approach) that guides how you do your work? Your leadership philosophy is the theory, attitude, or perspective that determines how you carry out your work. It is always operating in the background as impetus for your actions, ideas, attitudes, decisions, and expectations. Even if you are not able to articulate your philosophy, others around you can describe it based on your behavior and thought patterns.

Some leaders adopt a philosophy based on their past experiences—imitating the habits, approach, and demeanor of a past supervisor or an admired leader. Unfortunately, that is not always ideal since many leaders are passing on antiquated styles. Also, imitating someone else's approaches may not come across as authentic for you.

Exercise: Clarify your leadership philosophy.

This is a multi-step exercise to help you formulate your own leadership philosophy. It considers your values, beliefs, perspectives, and knowledge, along with people and organizational influences.

1. Start by considering the **values** you hold. Values are beliefs or ways of being we each hold as essential. We should not only know them, but also work to bring our behaviors into fidelity with them.

Look at this sample list of core values. Add others that come to mind.

integrity	transparency	trustworthy	spiritual
responsibility	caring	genuine	camaraderie
role model	empathy	faith	service
belonging	optimism	altruism	justice
commitment	inclusion	Intentional	dedication
respect	encourager	humor	fun
work ethic	honesty	supportive	kindness
love	fairness	partner	equality
achievement	loyalty	honesty	duty
Add Others			

These are my top 5, and here is what they look like at work.

My top five values	How they show up in my behaviors
1.	
2.	
3.	
4.	
5.	

2. Next, examine the **Assumptions** you hold about people.

To help formulate a personal leadership philosophy statement, take a moment, and write down just two assumptions or viewpoints you hold about people at work. For instance, *do you assume the best or worst about people? Do you assume only a few people are incredibly talented and the rest are just biding their time? Do you assume people can or cannot be trusted to do their jobs? Do you assume employees are well-intentioned and can be trusted to do their jobs without always standing over them? etc.* I assume....

1.
2.
3.

Think about the extent to which these align with your values. (Not all assumptions are helpful and should be re-examined periodically.)

3. Now, take a few moments to draft a sentence or two on your **leadership philosophy**, an anchoring statement that reflects your values, beliefs, and how you want to be seen as a leader.

Some examples I came across:

- *People have abundant capacity to create life-changing impact and my job is to provide them with support, tools, inspiration, and direction.*
- *I lead others with a focus on inspiring and planning around what is possible together even when things seem impossible.*
- *My aim is to guide and encourage people and be an available, approachable leader. Honesty, work ethic, loyalty, and respect are important. I will lead with strength, not to instill fear. At the same time, I will not tolerate unethical behavior or lackluster work from those I lead.*

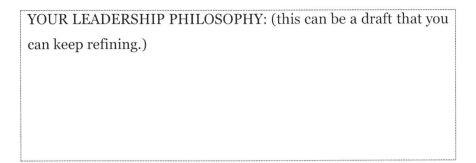

YOUR LEADERSHIP PHILOSOPHY: (this can be a draft that you can keep refining.)

Your philosophy can change over time as the leadership situation you find yourself in changes and requires something different to be highly effective. That does not mean you relinquish your values (though they can also evolve over time), just aspects of your approach.

ADDRESS YOUR SELF-AWARENESS GAP

"Those who know much about others may be smart, but those who understand themselves are even wiser." Lao Tsu

Get acquainted with your strengths and self-limiting habits. I often hear from my coaching clients that what they value most about our engagement is the emphasis on helping them see themselves and their thinking more clearly. This helps them choose actions to show up and lead in ways better aligned with their intentions. I find that leaders tend to either pay little attention to honoring their profound strengths, or they fail to examine the habitual, unhelpful patterns of behavior and beliefs that hinder their and their team's success.

Exercise: Inventory your Strengths: *What are my current skills and strengths* (areas where you stand out among peers)? Don't worry about sounding overconfident. Write as many as you can.

Accomplishments: What are my accomplishments over the last 12 months (major and smaller) that I have or have not celebrated? Write at least five (5) below, then pause a moment to honor all you do to demonstrate your worthiness for your role.

There are numerous assessment tools (e.g., DISC, StrengthsFinder, etc.) and people that can be helpful as you look at how to maximize your work results by using more of what you are already good at. Listen for cues from colleagues, staffers, and friends who give you hints about your strengths. They see you and know you.

What have you heard people consistently say you are good at?
(Maybe you have ignored them, but now is the time to take note.)

Ultimately, as we increase self-awareness, we want to know the degree of congruence between how we see ourselves and how others perceive and relate to us. Then we can choose to change or adapt specific behaviors (becoming an even better version of ourselves).

Being in touch with your strengths is not just about you; it also helps you distinguish yours from those of your direct reports. You can then grasp that the "If I can do it, they can too" mantra is illogical. Your journey then becomes discovering the different, even complementary talents others bring to the work. Another value in attending to your strengths is learning how and when (and when not) to use them.

I collaborated with a leader who, through several assessments, was able to see that she was highly competent in these emotional skills: influencing others, building bonds, handling conflict, achievement orientation and integrity. We spent time talking about how she might leverage these people skills to raise issues directly (which she had avoided) to help the leadership team examine scattershot, misaligned efforts that made it harder for them to get things done. With renewed confidence that people would recognize her sincerity when using her voice to influence needed change, she initiated healthy conflict to put issues on the table. And with her achievement drive she kept the issues front and center and the team established and agreed to new ways of working together.

Uncovering blind spots can help overcome limiting behaviors. Our eyes are not built to see everything. B*lind spots are areas that are blocked from a person's view.* **We cannot fully see ourselves in the same way we observe others.** Some areas that others may observe about us that we might not see include our *biases and beliefs, body language, idiosyncrasies, well-worn habits, viewpoints and values, instinctive responses, emotional messages, and more.*

Blind spots, unaddressed, can lead to self-deception: Because there are limits to our ability to see ourselves fully, if we are not trying to uncover these blind spots, we can become inclined towards self-deception. This tendency to *convince ourselves into believing false notions about ourselves despite evidence to the contrary,* is particularly problematic for leaders.

Three signs that you could be in a **state of self-deception** include:

- Looking for someone or something to blame for mistakes without seeing your part in the situation.
- Responding to setbacks more reactively than proactively, more defensively than receptively.
- Tending to overestimate your skills and dismissing or underestimating the effect of your shortcomings on others.
- Using lengthy rationalizations, explaining your "rightness."

"It [self-deception] blinds us to the true cause of problems, and once blind, all of the 'solutions' will actually make matters worse...To the extent we are self-deceived, our leadership is undermined at every turn." [1] P. viii

[1] The Arbinger Institute. 2000. Leadership and self-deception.

Some of us tend to think we're better than we really are. Reflect for a moment on four areas[2] from a 2017 report pinpointing areas where leaders deceive themselves into believing they are good, while employees report serious shortcomings:

- ☑ Genuine listening
- ☑ Showing appreciation
- ☑ Admitting mistakes
- ☑ Being honest with themselves and others

Exercise: *Choose at least one of these ways to uncover blind spots:*

- ❍ Expose yourself to newer information and perspectives (this can create "ahas"... things you didn't know you didn't know). Read, network, seek experts and innovators' views, etc.
- ❍ Ask yourself: What are 1-2 pieces of feedback I have heard that I ignored? How might they possibly reveal a blind spot?

- ❍ Complete behavioral style or skill assessments to increase your self-awareness.
- ❍ What is a new area of work that makes you a bit anxious? Perhaps there are some requirements or tasks that you

[2] Dale Carnegie & Associates, Inc. Recognizing Leadership Blind Spots. Wp_050817

haven't faced before. What are those? Identify people who can help you uncover what you need to know and do differently.

- Think of a situation that did not go as well as you'd like. What behaviors might have made it better? What skill, if you had it, would have been helpful? Who can you ask for feedback?

- Ask a trusted colleague for honest responses to two questions: *When I'm at my best, what do I do and how do I behave? When I'm not at my best, what do I do and how do I behave?*

- Pursue "truth" through staff feedback: Include direct and anonymous ways to ask your direct reports: *What is working well in my approach and support? What would you like to see change? What ideas do you have for me to better support you to help you do your best work?*

- Create a feedback habit. After meetings, presentations, events you lead, seek feedback for continuous improvements.

Be careful of over-applying your strengths: The old saying "too much of a good thing" applies to leaders too. As noted earlier, areas of blindness are not necessarily related to deficiencies since people can be oblivious to their strengths as well. The point is, if you are blind to your traits and behaviors, whether good or bad, they can be self-limiting. If you have been strong in being direct and assertive, there are instances where that behavior might not be as useful as in other settings. Tone down that strength situationally. Take time to determine which of your strengths are additive and which are not useful at a given time. Over-engaging certain strengths can come across as "too much" for a new work setting or team.

I can recall several leaders who faltered for this reason: Relying upon one or more of their strengths, which proved not particularly useful at the time or at least to the degree they were using them.

The next section is also related to how you engage your talents. It examines "how am I showing up?"

ALIGN YOUR LEADERSHIP PRESENCE

When you walk into a room, lead or participate in a meeting, or engage with staff and colleagues, what messages do you think you are conveying to everyone? How do they see you as a leader? Credible? Influential? Inspiring? Prepared? Caring? Committed? Or the opposite of any of these?

A frequent area of leaders' unawareness is related to showing up in ways that unknowingly diminish their credibility with peers and direct reports. This creates a perception gap between how we think we are presenting ourselves and how others see us based on our actions and attitudes. The skill of being aware of "how you show up" is attainable and referred to as leadership (executive or professional) presence. It is to *comfortably, confidently, and authentically send powerful, observable signals reflecting high quality engagement, alignment, inspiration, and motivation for people to act.* (modified from a definition at www.bates-communication.com)

Leaders with unrefined presence may appear to others to lack the attributes to lead well, even though they may be highly competent.

Read the story below that highlights one leader's *presence* gap:

> *There was a new and skilled educational leader who had a pattern of emotional volatility when staff failed to follow through on their work. She'd yell, demand, scold publicly, show negative facial expressions, etc. Staff soon became intimidated and would not speak up for fear of being castigated by this leader. What was lost was not only respect from her direct reports but also access to ground-level intelligence about the "goings on" in the organization.*
>
> *This client worked hard to improve her leadership presence, after recognizing that if her staffers were intimidated and fearful, she could not lead them well, they would not feel free enough to do their best work, and she was cut off from access to critical information.*

This leader hadn't given much thought to the type of "*presence*" the new role, culture, people dynamics, and responsibilities required, different from her previous role. In time, she decreased the gap between what she intended to convey to her team ("strong, confident, capable and committed leader") and what she was *conveying*, i.e., others' perceptions ("tyrannical, know-it-all, ego-driven leader").

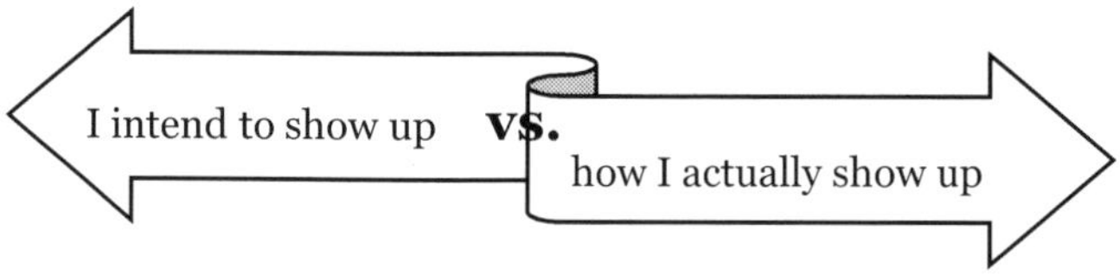

Reflection Exercise: Models of leadership presence generally focus on three broad questions. Write your response to each below. (Keep in mind that what's most important is to have those you lead complete this as well to determine what perception gaps may exist.)

1. What message do you send through your physical **style** and manner of communication?

2. What does the **substance** (experience-based knowledge, confidence, and composure) of your messages say to people about you as a leader?

3. What does your way of managing your emotions and perspectives say to people about your **character**?

The Bates Model of Executive Presence (ExPI)™ is a general rubric to help explore how we show up. It offers a chance to align our desired public presence with our actual behavior.

Caveat: I and many others are keenly aware and affected by views of executive presence that are dismissive of or devalue the variations of the authentic voice and style of under-represented groups, such as women and people of color. So, keep in mind, personal presence should never diminish your unique voice or cultural characteristics (e.g., The Crown Act is legally fighting hair discrimination related to African American hairstyles and texture in the workplace). The model's three dimensions (below) will look different for people, based on their individual attributes, so there is room to find yourself.

1. **CHARACTER.** This is the most foundational level of who you are as a person. Of the three dimensions, character is the **least observable**. It includes such aspects as *genuineness, courage, optimism, integrity, restraint, concern, humility, and priorities.* Leaders need to not only identify and clarify personal values but behave in accordance with them.

2. **SUBSTANCE** (also referred to as gravitas or command) is **cultivated over time**. It encompasses *practical wisdom, accumulated knowledge, maturity, confidence, strategic thinking, composure,* and *being attuned to the needs of others.* If leaders have style but not substance, they may be perceived as "empty suits."

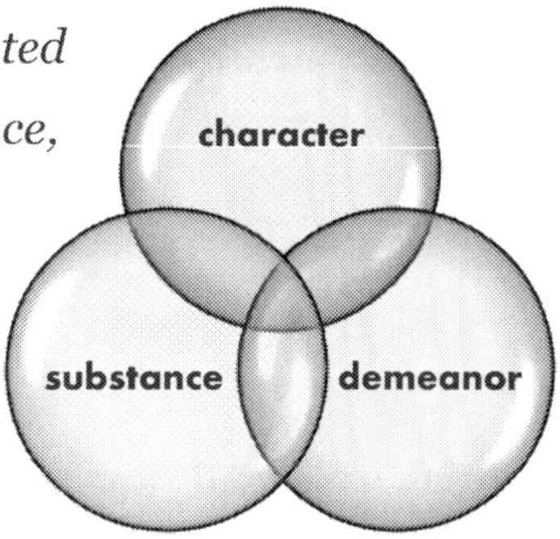

3. **DEMEANOR** is the **most visible**, "first impression" or "style" behaviors related to a leader's messaging. It is based on *mannerisms, assertiveness, appearance, inclusiveness, interpersonal dialogue quality, tactfulness, and how focused a leader is.* Style issues may prevent people from appreciating

a leader's substance and character. People may "tune out" a leader based purely on observations about style.

Reflection Questions:

1. Who comes to mind when you think of someone who demonstrates leadership presence? (people you know and/or public figures). And what do they do to show it?

 ----

2. What behaviors or attributes have you seen that detract from good *presence* (think of people you know who are talented...but)?

Exercise: My Leadership Presence. Rate 1 through 5 (based on what you believe you present to others) using this key:

1. I pay little attention to this.
2. I give some attention to this but need to do much better.
3. I'm OK with this, somewhat neutral.
4. Most people would agree this is a trait of mine.
5. People see this as a definite part of my identity as a leader.

1.	People likely see me as real, authentic, open, present, and sincere in my relations with others. (Character)	
2.	People would say I act with integrity, in alignment with my values and beliefs—living up to high standards. (Character)	
3.	People likely see me as demonstrating experience-based insight, practical wisdom, and knowledge that lead to good judgement and decision-making. (Substance)	
4.	My peers and staffers would agree that I have an inspiring vision of the future, backed by knowledge of key trends, and strategies to achieve the vision. (Substance)	

5. People would say I look, show up, and act like an able leader—in my appearance, posture, timeliness, energy I project and the tactful way I manage situations (Demeanor)	
6. People see me as demonstrating interest in others, concern, and promoting a culture that values others. (Character)	
7. People likely see me as being self-assured in decision-making and action and someone who accepts responsibility for my actions. (Substance)	
8. People see me as someone who is intentional in clarifying the focus and keeping things on track, while being open to dissent and willing to change course as needed. (Demeanor)	
9. People see me as one who resonates with others, being attentive, attuned, and responsive to others' feelings and thoughts. (Substance)	
10. People would say that I demonstrate humility by indicating I am aware of my strengths and weaknesses, and I act from a belief that all people have worth. (Character)	
11. People would say I display a calm disposition, including restraint, reasonableness and avoidance of emotional extremes or impulsiveness. (Character)	
12. People know me to actively involve others, welcome diverse points of view, and listen well. (Demeanor)	
13. People see me as a leader who is calm, composed, and steady in crisis and able to calm and re-focus others. (Substance)	
14. My coworkers would say I speak up, share my thoughts, and raise issues directly, valuing productive conflict and without alienating others. (Demeanor)	

Action Plan: Aligning My Intended and Actual Presence

Using your ratings above, list on the next page, the item numbers that show the ways you think you are demonstrating leadership presence, then the ways you would like to show up differently.

Areas where I am showing up well	

Areas for adjustments	

My Next Steps for Better Presence (1-2 only):

1.

2.

MIND YOUR MOOD, ENERGY AND WELL-BEING

The mood and energy state of the leader has a ripple effect on the entire team, referred to as *emotional contagion.* A leader who is emotionally steady helps create steadiness in the environment. An optimistic leader will lighten the tension during challenges; they are genuine in exuding life-giving energy rather than life-depleting. Pessimistic leaders can establish an environment characterized by fear, anxiety, worst case scenario thinking and low creativity.

Moods and energy states are similar. They are about the leader's temperament and tone—their overall state of mind or feeling.

"A leader's miserable mood can sap the energy out of a room, even a virtual one. It can unnerve people, cause unnecessary anxiety, and affect productivity. Positive emotional contagion, on the other

hand, can result in improved cooperation, decreased conflict, and better performance."[3]

Generally, it is good to take note of the moods of those around you to adapt as appropriate. Too much rah-rah energy in times of distress fails to motivate and can come across as superficial or naïve.

I observed this with a leader who was super charged all the time. During the Covid19 pandemic, when staffers were worried about their loved ones, managing their kids during virtual school for months, concerned about staying safe, the "all is great with the world" energy of this leader created a sense of detachment and inauthenticity (as a direct report shared with him). In other words, his "motivation" did not motivate.

Resonance--being in tune with how others are feeling—matters. It allows you to offer them a measure of hopefulness about what can be.

Exercise: Mood and Energy

1. My mood at work is generally which of these? (Mark 1 or 2)

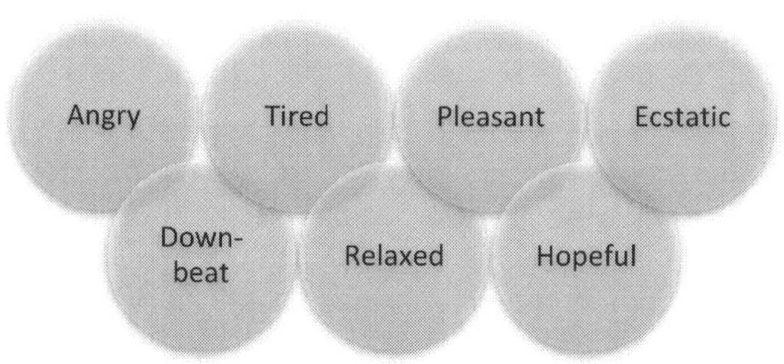

[3] Martinuzee, B. 2020. https://www.mindtools.com/blog/moods-moody-leaders-and-how-not-to-be-one/

2. What is a recent example of a situation that reflects the influence of my energy or mood on others?

---

3. How can I be a role model for mood and energy management so the team can focus more positively on their work and not get stressed due to my moods?

Tips to improve your energy state:

☑ Prioritize getting enough rest, exercise, and emotional replenishment.

☑ Practice steadiness, i.e., model mood stability for your direct reports; practice positive self-management during stress.

☑ Enhance your emotional intelligence; read about it, take an assessment, and create an action plan that enhances emotional competencies such as *realistic optimistic, stress management, and emotional self-regulation.*

☑ Bring your best to stressful situations, which might mean--pause, pull yourself together, and put on your game face.

- ☑ Take rejuvenation breaks, especially on days that are long, filled with meetings. Give yourself 10-15 minutes to breathe, stretch, and recharge.
- ☑ Don't send strong messages until you feel re-centered.
- ☑ Be honest about the challenges facing the team, remind them that you are also affected, yet set a tone that "we will get through this together."

Well-being as a factor in workplace performance. The state of your overall wellness affects the energy and mindset you bring to work. Even with a positive demeanor, without habits that keep you centered, refreshed, and grounded, your strengths will play out in less-than-optimal ways. Such missteps can reverberate widely because leaders impact others.

One executive client was grappling with the staff's diminished emotional wellness during the 2020-2023 Covid 19 pandemic. Committed to adapting regular practices to allow staff to address emotional healthiness, she assumed performance would decrease as a trade-off. I encouraged her not to assume well-being and performance were either/or propositions since studies reveal that supporting well-being fosters high performance. At the least, attending to the staff's physical, emotional and job well-being can motivate them to bring a better version of themselves to their work.

Organizations that have staff wellness integrated into their strategic priorities describe these as benefits: staff taking fewer sick days, higher performance, lower rates of burnout, and higher retention. I saw it stated simply in this way: ***"When employee wellbeing improves, performance improves too."***

Consider staff wellness across various areas of life. Think about *sense of belonging, spiritual states, stress levels, outside relaxing pursuits, feelings of safety, sense of hope, physical wellness, relationships, raising children, hobbies,* and others. A deficit in any of these can have adverse effects on the work atmosphere and the work itself since people may underperform and make uncharacteristically poor decisions when emotional well-being suffers.

When you are well and are an advocate for wellness, your staff will appreciate it and likely see overall life improvements.

Exercise: Activating Wellbeing. Four Questions

1. What do you do to get back to your center, to a state of balance?	
2. What are your preferred health/wellbeing practices? How well do you stick to them?	
3. And to what extent do you inquire about and foster the same with your direct reports?	
4. How flexible are you regarding modifying workplace practices to support well-being for your team members?	

Exercise: Mapping Well-Being

Based on what Gallup[4] describes as the five key areas of well-being, place a rating of 1-5 (1 is the lowest and 5 the highest) on the map below in each category to assess your current well-being state.

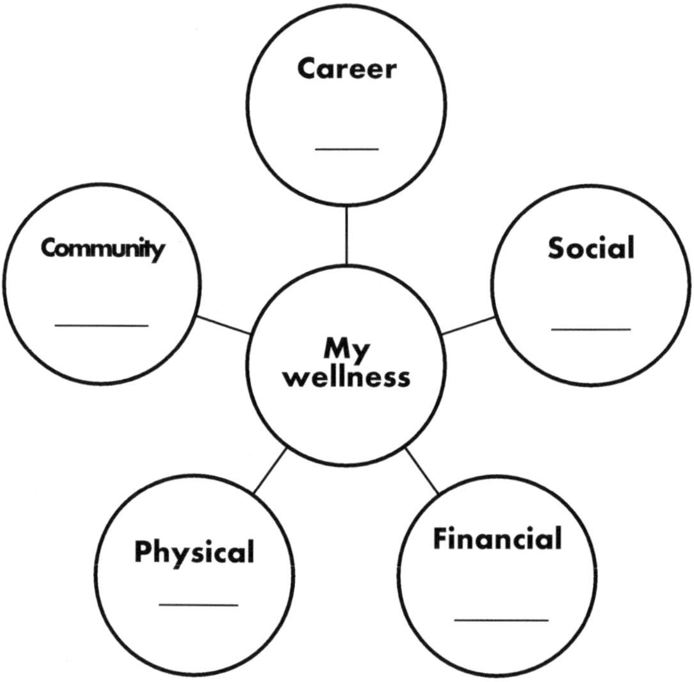

Action: What are two fairly easy things you can do to increase your thriving in any of these five areas of well-being?

1. ______________________________

2. ______________________________

---

[4] Gallup.com. 10 Well-being practices to guide leaders. 5/7/2021.

BECOME A MORE AGILE THINKER

In today's dynamic work environment, every leader needs to think more expansively. Broadening one's perspective is key to effectively leading others. Though this sounds like common sense, coming to the realization that your way is *not* the only way remains a central theme in my work with middle and top-level leaders. In reality, for some leaders, the higher up they ascend, the more resolute they are that their way is the best and only way.

Mental agility is a signature strength for a leader. It is key to collaboration and inclusion and allows leaders and organizations to unlock the talents and creativity of their people as they address their complex issues. This means building your capacity to flex, adapt, expand your thinking and acting. This adaptability is an indicator of higher levels of emotional intelligence, good listening skills, and ease with integrating new perspectives.

Take this story of a nonprofit senior leader. As we wrapped up our coaching engagement, she was full of energy as she shared how unstuck and re-motivated she became once she arrived at one insight—that she was trapped in her own way of thinking.

> *"It became clear that I came into this new job thinking things should go the way I've always seen them. I had an inflexible way of thinking. I am excited to be more agile and accept that ambiguity is not necessarily a terrible thing. My new openness to see other ways of doing things has made me more empathetic and helped my relationships with my colleagues and my manager."*

Look at two ways to adapt and expand your thinking.

1. ***Integrate new perspectives***. When there are multiple people in a room, there are bound to be multiple perspectives (unless you're an insecure leader who fosters "group think" and staffers are afraid to express an opinion unlike that of their leader). Additionally, as you develop your skills, you will inevitably come across new and different viewpoints. Regardless of how it happens, integrating new perspectives means thoughtfully considering what you can gain from different thought patterns to enhance your thinking and perceptions.

   Genuinely reflect on: *How well do I make space for other viewpoints? Do I overtalk or block people's voices or get defensive?* Incorporating new perspectives requires intention and practice until you come to see its rewards.

   One of the biggest barriers to overcome in working with people is helping them shift from vehemently defending their stance and blaming others to considering alternative ways to view situations.

   When your interaction with others is challenging, try asking yourself: *How might (name of the other person) be experiencing the situation?* This helps you build the maturity to recognize there are other ways to view and interpret the same experience, and taking that into account, helps move towards resolution and learning.

Here are suggestions to begin opening yourself to different or new perspectives with your direct reports:

a. Invite team members to offer their views.

b. Be silent as you allow the team to wrestle with issues. Then help them reach consensus to resolve the issues.

c. Formulate action plans around decisions that were derived from combining perspectives.

2. ***Practice Reframing***: Applying the reframing technique can improve your thinking and problem solving. To reframe is to reconceptualize a problem or situation by seeing it from a different or unfamiliar perspective.

"Altering the conceptual or emotional context of a problem often serves to alter perceptions of the problem's difficulty and to open up possibilities for solving it." (from the American Psychological Association's dictionary)

I partnered with a leader who had decided her new supervisor was untrustworthy, conniving, self-serving, and out to get her after only three weeks on the job. (Her supervisor had only been hired a few weeks before her.) I prompted her to reframe her thinking to consider what might be some issues he was facing in his new role.

Our conversation went something like this:

Me: *"Think about this "new" top leader who just started and who was offered little onboarding to acclimate him to the culture or organization. What might be driving him to behave in ways you believe are about self-interest?"*

Client: (after taking a breath and trying to set aside her view for a moment): *"It must be tough on him. He's trying to figure out who's who? What's what? and how to be a valuable player around here without having received much guidance."*

Me: *"Then how might you go into your meeting more open minded and with better emotional self-regulation?" (She had a pretty explosive, accusatory exchange with him the week prior.)*

Client: *"I can go in with the intent to understand him, what he brings to the work since I know he is very smart and how he'd like us to work together on our goals."*

Client: *"My mindset will be 'This is going to be a productive meeting that brings us in greater alignment as workmates'."*

Reframing (viewing the situation differently) seemed to help her, and it eased her anxiety. The practice of reframing requires leaders to manage their emotions in a mature manner.

Reframing your views requires intention and practice for you to reap the benefit of unfreezing your unhelpful thought patterns and allowing better ones to emerge.

Exercise: Practice Reframing

1. What is a situation that I am addressing that reframing might be helpful (i.e., shifting to a different view of the situation)?

2. How serious is this? Am I getting worked up over nothing?

3. What can I change about how I view the problem, which could at least somewhat change how I feel about it?

4. How can I manage things differently--so I can direct my emotional energy to bigger, more critical issues?

Same problem. Different perspective.

IMPROVE RECEPTIVITY TO FEEDBACK AND COACHING

Leaders expend much of their energy on external issues, including supporting the needs of colleagues and direct reports. That's the job. Those who have evolved their skills have switched from "bossing" to leading their people by doing more coaching and development. Leaders can also use these practices on themselves to good effect. Whether you use an external coach or self-coaching, it is hugely helpful to the leader to remain receptive to growing.

"Coaching is valuable because none of us transform our thinking on our own. Humans are masters at rationalizing

> *hastily made choices no matter how logical we think we are. We're also exceptional at blaming whomever or whatever we can when those choices turn out badly. We don't change well on our own. To stop adverse thinking patterns, someone outside our head needs to disrupt our thinking by reflecting our thoughts back to us and asking questions that prompt us to wonder why we think the way we do."*[5]

Show up as coachable. Coachability has been named one of the top leader superpowers. A coachable leader has an ongoing growth orientation and is someone who possesses *"enough confidence to learn more and enough humility to want to."* from Coachability: The Leadership Superpower[6] It includes seeking, being open to, applying feedback, and possessing a willingness to re-assess beliefs.

These words from a client to their human resources executive demonstrated coachability:

> *"My three months of leadership coaching has been instrumental in identifying strengths to lean into and uncovering what were previously blind spots. I truly believe the coaching has been beneficial and that there is more that can be accomplished with coaching to aid me in serving this organization."*

Self-coaching: You can apply self-coaching to navigate many of the situations you face, build healthier self-awareness, and improve self-regulation. Practicing introspective inquiry builds your capacity for

---

[5] Reynolds, M. 2020. Coach the Person, not the Problem. P. 20
[6] Wilde, K. 2023. P. 21.

self-correction (to observe how you are doing and make corrections) and *self-generation* (to renew yourself, adjust your thinking, release unhelpful or unverified assumptions, and move forward).

Learn to climb down the "Ladder of Inference." A framework to foster self-correction can help you see when you are making unhelpful assumptions, imagining intentions, creating meaning, or making decisions based on your own internal construction of "truth." Called the **Ladder of Inference**, (created in 1974)[7], it assists us with discerning the disparity between actual data (facts) and beliefs we form about them. I've used this visual (at right) with clients to help them re-think situations in a more constructive way.

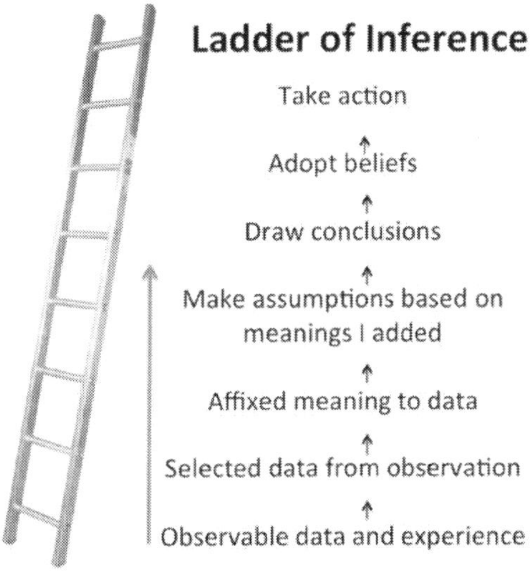

Here's one example of the benefit of climbing down a few rungs of the ladder*: One client spoke about a colleague who would disagree with her views about work situations in meetings (***observable data***). *She focused more on the dissent and tone and not the content* **(selected a piece of the data)** *to decide this means the colleague thinks she (the client) doesn't know what she's talking about*

[7] Argyris, C. 1974. See The Fifth Discipline, Peter Senge. 1990.

(affixed meaning). *This then inferred to my client "she dislikes me and is trying to undermine me"* **(draw conclusions).** *From there, the client construed every interaction thereafter to be "proof" that her assumptions were true* **(adopted belief).** *Their relationship continued deteriorating, and she treated the colleague dismissively or confrontationally* **(take action).** *The work was for her to see there may be other reasons for her disagreeing, and there might be some useful suggestions embedded in her dissent. Coming down the ladder and reframing helped improve their working relationship.*

A few more simple examples (all unconfirmed assumptions):

- *He didn't eat the food I cooked, so he thinks I can't cook.*
- *She was frowning when she walked by me, so she is mad at me.*
- *He looked at his phone during my presentation, I must not be very good at this.*

Can you think of a current situation where you need to evaluate your assumptions (climb down the Ladder of Inference) to have more productive interactions? ______________________________

____

____

All of us make assumptions, and we couldn't get through life without them. The thing to remember is they are assumptions, not facts. When they get you into messy territory, it's time to check your reasoning and beliefs. You can coach or coax yourself *down the ladder* to rethink your circumstances to make more thoughtful decisions and improve interactions with a colleague or direct report.

Now, shifting back to self-coaching, try using this six-question framework to address an issue you are currently facing.

Exercise: Practice self-coaching. Examine your thought processes then bring your thoughts and actions into alignment.

Here's an example. A blank worksheet is at the end of this chapter for you to use for reflection as issues emerge.

1. **Identify the situation and desired outcomes**. What specific issue or problem do I need to solve?

Ex. I want to manage my emotions better (be calmer and open to feedback) when meeting with my supervisor

2. **Reflect**: Where am I now with this issue? How well am I doing or not doing? How are my actions or mindset interfering with me resolving this issue? Is how I view the situation an issue?

Ex. I get anxious when my supervisor even hints that I've made a mistake. I think I'm about 3 out 10 on emotional management. I keep over-reacting, stressing myself, and giving the impression that I'm fragile.

3. What are a few **options** for handling this situation? List a few and place an X by the one that resonates most.

Ex. x I could do relaxing breaths before and during our meetings and have a "be calm" post it note I can privately see.
Ask for more clarity before a task to understand his view of success.
Be sure I'm rested and centered before our conversations to show up differently.
xPractice better emotional management in other areas as well to get better.

4. I **plan** to implement this option by doing and/or being...

Ex. Prepare my mind for both positive and corrective feedback when we next meet, affirming both will be helpful. Then say, "Thanks, that was helpful."

5. **Act** on the plan, paying attention to any items in #4. How is it going? How are you holding yourself accountable?

Ex. I'm getting better. I am calmer and come in relaxed, which seems to make it easier for him to talk to me. I still need to take the time to prepare myself right before our meetings.

6. **Reflect, celebrate**, continue until the new habits stick.

Ex. When I was calm, pleasant and open, it went well. I realized I had been only paying attention to the minor corrective feedback and not the positives. He actually thinks overall I'm good. I'll keep this practice up.

Your feedback receptivity. Assess your network to find ways to garner feedback and support. Everyone needs others in their circle for support and growth. That could mean a professional association, personal board of directors, a cheerleading friend, or a work mentor. We each need a place to release frustrations, learn, seek, and receive feedback, and celebrate ourselves. (See Chapter 7 on Feedback and apply relevant ideas and practices to your own feedback habits.)

Exercise: Who's on my feedback and support team? In the space below jot down names or groups who can offer new insights or useful feedback.

☑ Who can provide knowledge, resources and new and alternative insights about navigating your specific role?

☑ Who can offer perspectives about the culture and "politics" of the organization, and offer feedback on how they believe you are managing within that culture?

☑ Who are your honest, trusting confidantes who know you well and with whom you can share opportunities and anxieties, and they in turn can offer gentle feedback?

Leveraging the *right* people for your learning and feedback network can make a vast difference in how you lead yourself and others.

Closing Journal—Notes to Self on Leading Myself

Reminder: This chapter addressed six areas for leading yourself: *Clarify your leadership beliefs and philosophy, enhance self-awareness, align your presence, address your mood and well-being, become a more agile thinker, and prioritize learning and receptivity to feedback.* This chapter is one you will benefit from revisiting from time to time on your leadership journey.

Chapter 2, the next LEAD KEY chapter, examines the higher-level skills and attributes needed to lead and achieve for the organizational unit for which you are responsible.

Blank Self-Coaching Worksheet and Process

1. **Identify the situation and desired outcomes**. What specific issue or problem do I need to solve?
2. **Reflect**: Where am I now in this specific area? How well am I doing or not? How are my actions or mindset interfering with me resolving this issue? Is the way I'm viewing the situation getting me the results I want?
3. What are a few **options** (3-4) for managing this situation? List a few and place an X by the one that resonates most.
4. I **plan** to implement this option by doing and/or being...
5. **Act** on the plan, paying attention to any items in #4. How is it going? How are you holding yourself accountable?
6. **Reflect, celebrate**, continue until the new habits stick.

Chapter 2

Lead Your UNIT

Six essentials for leading your area:

1. Build organizational level skills.
2. Allocate time to lead your people.
3. Lead your people with a coherent vision and strategy.
4. Get ahead of and interpret organizational changes.
5. Be a champion of goal clarity and aligned decision-making.
6. Monitor your inspiration quotient.

BUILD YOUR ORGANIZATIONAL LEVEL SKILLS

Leading others capably requires a practice of seeking new knowledge and skills related to your specific industry. Remarked Jim Kouzes, renowned leadership author and professor, about his research:

> *"We find that higher performing leaders more frequently engage in learning activities than do lower performing leaders.[8]"*

Too many leaders neglect or deprioritize seizing opportunities to turn their potential into the higher-level skills needed for an increasingly complex operating environment. If you or the organization is focused on offering the best products or services in finance, education, human resources, consumer goods, community services, marketing, etc., monitoring the external landscape to keep pace with the new

---

[8] Duncan, R. D., Forbes.com, April 7, 2018, Leadership as dialogue, not monologue.

technologies, trends, and inventive practices is essential to leading others capably.

There are many prices to be paid when a leader operates with a static or limited skillset. Among them are:

- *Staffers will function far beneath their potential.*
- *Employees are more likely to leave.*
- *Customers may go elsewhere—to more relevant, responsive, and value-adding competitors.*
- *The leader's problem-solving abilities stagnate.*
- *Operating deficits can mount and cause reductions in force.*
- *You may feel high stress and a sense of being directionless.*

Mind your expertise gap: No matter how competent you may be in one role, when the environment or goals change, a gap can open between your current skills and the new ones needed to be successful. Stay in the growth mode: Assess and elevate your skills and mindset.

Ascending to a new role? The next two pages are from my *The Everyday Leader* book. These pages make the case for minding the expertise gaps that arise as you start a new job.

How did you rise to your current leadership assignment? What factors converged to bestow upon you the honor of leading others? The responses influence how you need to prepare for a new role.

A sizeable number of today's leaders have been *Thrust into Leadership*, that is, they became what's referred to as *Accidental*

Leaders. That type of new leader traveled through one or a combination of the first five of **six ascension pathways** listed here:

1. selected based on their *potential* to do the job (e.g., interest, commitment, and education).
2. they performed well as *individual contributors* (excellent in a subject matter expert role that didn't require leading others).
3. as a reward for time served in a previous job, *deserving* of upward movement as a retention strategy.
4. had the right connections and was championed by someone with the influence to get them the job (e.g., inheriting a family business or benefiting from the *friend network*.)
5. *no one else* wanted to lead, often the case in volunteer or hard to fill roles (so a less-preferred candidate wins the job).
6. intentionally *prepared* to lead others at a higher level.

Those in category 6 might have arrived at their roles 1) as a result of a succession planning *process* (not just succession identification); 2) used a targeted development plan; 3) engaged in structured mentoring, coaching or shadowing efforts; 4) worked with the hiring supervisor to develop a thorough onboarding, culture integration and transition plan; or 5) took the initiative to engage in self-study.

Neither of the first five patterns is inherently good or bad; they are just that—patterns that may indicate the need for the new hire to plan approaches for success, rather than just do what they've always done.

Reflection: Consider the six ascension patterns. Which do you believe best reflects how you arrived at your current role? It may be a combination of factors. ______________________________

____

When hastily assigned or elevated into roles that require people to lead others, the leader's (and the organization's) inattention to effective transition planning can result in unfortunate outcomes. You can, however, take steps to ensure you are prepared to lead well.

Exercise: Skill Inventory

This exercise uses a set of general leadership competencies that prepare you to lead your business unit, your team and yourself well. Look at the list and rate yourself on each. This is a chance to take stock of the skills you already have so you can better deploy them and identify areas to prioritize for development. Focus on competencies that are impacting or will soon impact your work.

Rating: 5 strength+, 4 strong, 3-I'm Ok, 2-needs work; 1-a serious growth area

Priority: Place a check (✓) for those areas that really need attention because they affect your job, your well-being, or your team. Which should you prioritize for attention and development? Usually, if you work on just 1 or 2 areas, those will have a positive effect on several others.

Competency	Rating	Priority
Emotional self-management, i.e., *composure, self-control, resilience*		
Conflict resolution		
Results-focused		
Industry specific skills (continuously learning)		

Delegation		
Team building		
Problem solving		
Coaching and mentoring		
Leading change (processes)		
Interpersonal (people) skills, i.e., *communication, inclusion, empathy, collaboration*		
Managing projects		
Budget management		
Learning agility (growth oriented)		
Setting direction (strategic viewpoint)		
Decisiveness in decision-making		
Managing organizational politics		
Coalition building		
Work-life integration		

Write your 1-2 priority competency development areas: ________

____

Don't try too much at once: A study which said leaders need skills in a dozen+ areas *"revealed that leaders who excelled in 'focus on results' and 'interpersonal skills' had an 92% probability of being perceived as top tier leaders."*[9] These two areas made a difference!

[9] Zengerfolkman.com. The Extraordinary Leader eBook, p. 11. 2023.

ALLOCATE TIME TO LEAD YOUR PEOPLE

Everybody is busy, and we each prioritize what and who we think deserve our finite time. Allocating time to lead and engage with our staffers is correlated with getting the best work from each, yet attention to them can fall to the wayside in all the busyness. Think of ways you may be squandering time, such as 1) in wasteful, unfocused meetings, 2) overmanaging rather than developing team members, or 3) putting out unending fires and other less productive activities.

Parkinson's Law can make you feel justifiably too busy to do your leadership work. This 1942 "law" held that "*work expands so as to fill the time available for its completion.*" That means, if you assign yourself 10 hours to complete a task, you get it done in 10; if you give yourself 40 hours for the same task, you manage to take all 40 hours to do it. Overcome this habit by giving yourself less time, then get the task done. Spend that freed up time with your people.

An effective leader works *through* people not instead of or despite of them. They can visualize the straight line from their investment in developing, supporting, coaching, and connecting with their people to accomplishing the organization's goals.

Are you rising to your job? Are you a leader who was promoted to a higher level but continues to work at the lower level of your old job? I've had clients who had to "unlearn" their attachment to past work behaviors from a previous job. They became aware that they were spending too much time on in-the-weeds tasks (i.e., transactional).

Exercise: Time Allocation. Think about three types of work[10]:

Transactional: largely administrative that usually addresses needs of an individual; issues that need to be solved quickly.

Tactical: projects; planning and implementing solutions to support people in getting their work done (e.g., new work processes, technology, learning or other systems). Often this is a manager's role, though managers also might think strategically about their business unit or group.

Strategic: This longer-term work is tied to business goals, and effects and benefits the entire business unit. It will require tactical projects to be successful. (strategic work includes, for example, strategic planning, partnerships, financial viability, staff development, etc.)

> *"To think strategically is to allocate one's time effectively so it is productive. Unproductive time is spent putting out fires, reacting to urgent but unimportant matters, and working on misdirected strategies."* Rich Horwath, Strategic Thinking

Next, you will reflect on your time distribution and any needed shifts to enable more focus on leading the organization, developing your people, and planning for the future of the work.

1. Based on 100% of your time, indicate the estimated percentage you currently spend doing each type of work? (No right answer)

[10] Robinson, D., and Robinson. J. 2015. Performance Consulting. 3rd edition.

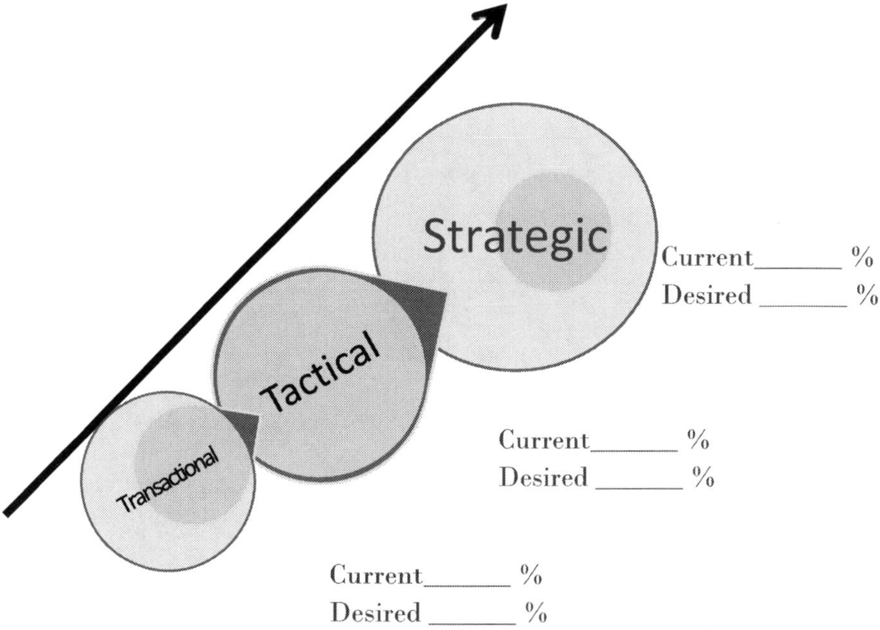

2. Now, enter the desired time percentages that allow you more time to focus on higher level work over the next six months.

3. What approaches might you use to **ALLOCATE** more of your time for higher level work (things to stop, start or delegate)?

LEAD WITH A COHERENT, INSPIRING VISION

Skillful leaders, responsible for setting direction for everyone's work, communicate the vision, goals, and priorities clearly, regularly, and powerfully. This signals to staff what to prioritize and the role their work plays in achieving the goals.

> *One long-term coaching client heads a nonprofit, and when I interviewed those on his senior team, neither of the eight could articulate exactly what the leader has as their current priorities. They were enmeshed in a culture of busyness as if their flurry of activity equated to accomplishment. They expressed varying degrees of frustration and requested I prod the leader to tell them "what's most important for us right now."*

Without a clear vision, communicated across the team or organization, a lot of wasted energy is expended by people working at cross purposes. People end up tired, confused, lacking a sense of purpose, and the goals seem to never reach completion.

Being clear about what the work is and why it matters is important for you and your team's ongoing inspiration and sense of purpose.

Exercise: Coherent Vision and Strategy

Try this activity to remind yourself of the purposefulness of the work.

1. How would you describe the WHY of your team and unit's work?

   ----

2. What are the roles you and your team play in achieving these important goals?

   ----

3. How do you share your vision for the work with the team? How often do you share it?

4. What are the steps or methods you are using with your team to help them succeed in their work?

(examples: knowledge sharing, financial efficiency, learning current trends, inclusiveness, responsiveness, trying novel approaches, engaging customers, etc.)

5. What are the standards for behavior that guide how people do their work and interact with each other? Are they known and reinforced?

Number 5 is a good and needed topic for team development conversations. (See Chapter 9 for more on this topic.)

CHANGE: ANTICIPATE, INTERPRET, COORDINATE

Inevitably, things will change in your organization as the world changes. In today's fast-paced context with so many technological breakthroughs (that few can keep up with), you will need to lead your direct reports to manage changing customer needs, trends in your industry, competition for clients and resources, internal restructures, and more.

Adaptability and *managing ambiguity* are now essential 21st Century leader attributes. Make sure you are on board with and know the business rationale for organizational changes. Adapt as needed, freeing yourself from the "we've always done it this way" mantra.

One of your functions is to lead change initiatives. You will do that at an elevated level if you are either CEO, president, or executive director. If you lead a department, your role is to implement the change by aligning your team's processes, systems, attitudes, and the culture with the new or redefined goals.

Since it is normal for people to think of change with trepidation, especially changes they don't understand or that they believe will adversely impact their lives, encourage your direct reports to become more change adaptable. This attitude can be a value-add for them as the changes unfold. Staffers who have been chronically negative and determined to infect others with that energy, during times of change, are often perceived as least valuable and easily expendable.

What is worse than avoiding change is leaving processes and cultural norms intact that are no longer useful. Some practices, even some you've loved, can become impediments to progress. Be discerning about what needs to stay and go. Train your mind to think about, even anticipate change, for the good of the organization and the team.

Exercise: Anticipate and Manage Change

1. What significant changes have you had to deal with at work over the last 6-12 months? (*Covid19 pandemic, economic trends, innovations, new products, work arrangements…*)

   ----

2. What is your typical response to changes that were initiated without your input?

    ---

3. What potentially anxiety-producing changes might occur at work over the next six to 12 months based on work and societal trends? Mark on the chart below.

Some common changes ✓			
Role restructuring/redesign		New line of business	
New leader/ new approach		Shift in priorities	
New partnerships		New work processes	
Workforce reductions		Work arrangements	
New technology installation		Well-being focus	
Other:		Other:	

4. What adjustments in the way you and your team do your work are needed to perform well in light of these potential changes?

    ---

5. How can you help your team be more open to change?

BE A CHAMPION OF GOAL CLARITY

Clarity can go a long way in getting the right work done, in the right way, making the best decisions, and achieving the best results. Staffers report over and over of being unclear on myriad issues: priorities, processes, acceptable behavior, policies, etc. How can you champion clarity then make decisions that align with those goals?

Have you sat in a meeting only to leave wondering what the purpose was, what the leader was trying to say, what you were supposed to do after the meeting, or what decisions were made? We all have. So, as simple as it sounds, clarity is important because other people depend on you bringing clarity for their success and direction for the work.

Exercise: Getting Clearer. These are simple Yes or No questions that might prompt you to refine your messaging to ensure clarity.

1. Is everyone clear on the department's current priorities?	Y___ N___
2. Do you ensure everyone is clear on how their job role connects to the overall goals?	Y___ N___
3. Are each person's goals jointly created, specific, clear, meaningful, and measurable?	Y___ N___
4. When a decision is made, is everyone clear that it has been made and what the decision is?	Y___ N___
5. Do you translate organizational messages to your team positively and clearly?	Y___ N___
6. In written communications to your team, are your messages purposeful, succinct, and clear?	Y___ N___
7. Are your communication protocols clear and known, with everyone informed and respected?	Y___ N___

Be clear on your own goals: Stop and ponder the question: *What am I trying to accomplish as I do my work every day?* This is a big question, that in the flurry of work tasks, can get lost. When the goal (s) is unclear, the team is lost, energy can wane, and stress can increase due to all the minor disconnected transactional tasks.

Think about what you and your team are trying to accomplish. You and your team's work ought to begin with goal clarity, which comes from you and serves as an anchor for the work everyone performs.

With all the tasks I/we do, I am aiming for them to add up to what? (your goal statement).

Note to self: What message can you tell yourself about demonstrating clarity in your dealings with staff, realizing there are consequences for the nature and quality of your messaging?

Decisiveness: Goal clarity is essential for effective decision-making. Decisiveness and decision-making are core leadership skills. When leaders are not internally clear of where they are headed, it incapacitates them to make effective decisions. Decisions should be aligned with the defined pathway. Despite the process you use for decision-making, it does little good when goals are ambiguous, and the leader lacks confidence and maturity to make thoughtful choices.

Too much collaboration and overanalyzing can waste time, frustrate staff, and look like leadership impotence. *Decisiveness is to make choices effectively, efficiently, and confidently.* It is informed by considering multiple options and a range of possible outcomes. It is guided by clarity of goals, values, and embracing a bit of risk and ambiguity.

I worked with a leadership team who *couldn't decide how to decide* major organizational issues. They spent thousands of dollars on consulting services to help them decide. Despite that, they went round and round and couldn't figure out who would make final decisions about budget cuts. The team was frustrated because no one would decide. What was missing was leadership; their sitting CEO lacked the skill and confidence to be decisive, rationalizing that he was using collaborative leadership. Anytime it costs a financially challenged organization tens of thousands of dollars that could have been used elsewhere, that's not collaboration, it's poor leadership.

In crisis, people value and have more confidence when a leader demonstrates decisiveness. Often decision-making requires: *clarity on what the decision is, specifying the expected outcome, gathering and analyzing information related to the decision, identifying alternatives, remaining open to diverse ideas, assessing and choosing the best path, making the decision, implementing, monitoring and mitigating risks, and adjusting as needed.* Then decisiveness follows where the leader, with confidence, is definitive in making the choices.

MONITOR YOUR INSPIRATION QUOTIENT.

According to a recent Zenger-Folkman leadership study including more than a million people[11], inspiring others was rated the most important skill employees desired from their leaders. Employees who viewed their leaders as *inspiring* experienced higher satisfaction and retention, efficiency, and performance than those led by the 76% of leaders who use a driving, demanding, and prodding style.

Despite the case for inspiration being identified as a critical leader attribute, there are managers who hold a belief that inspiration is the sole responsibility of the individual worker. I have heard more than once: *"It's not my job to motivate them to do what they are paid to do."* Sound familiar? The notion that a paycheck is inspiration enough is a flawed idea. ***Inspirational leaders know that they are aiming to ignite internal motivation for the job***. They know they are stimulating staffers to do their work without constant monitoring, where the team members are internally committed to making their contributions at an elevated level of quality.

Since the leader establishes the team's working environment, inspiration is a differentiator in how the team *feels* about their work. An uninspiring leader can deflate even their most committed staffer.

Inspirational and charismatic leadership are not the same thing. You don't have to be a motivational speaker to be inspirational. I have worked with some generally introverted, non-gregarious leaders who people felt inspired by because of other important attributes. One

[11] Zenger & Folkman, Inspiring in the New Era, 2022.

was lauded by his team as inspiring because of his unwavering passion for customers, attending to staff well-being, leading with vision, and modeling maturity during challenging times. Inspiring leaders amplify what's working and acknowledge "we are doing something meaningful together." They manage uncertainty well, allaying anxiety which frees people emotionally to do their work.

To what extent do you believe your team feels "inspired" by you as their leader when doing their work? Circle one.

Very inspired	Most are inspired	Mixed bag	Mostly just doing the job	Low or no inspiration

Inspiration traits vary. Employees are not all inspired by the same thing. For that reason, it might be useful to ask your direct reports: *What does it take for you to do your work with a full heart? What inspires deep engagement in your work over the long haul?*

Bain and Company developed an inspirational leadership model that includes 33 of the most powerful attributes.[12] They found that ***"inspired employees are twice as productive as satisfied employees."*** A positive note is that leaders need *distinctive* (better than most of their peers) strengths in any combination of **just four** of those 33 to show up as an inspirational leader, though one is non-negotiable—*Centeredness (fully engaged and present).*

What follows on the next page are groupings to summarize Bain's 33 inspirational attributes.

[12] Horwitch, M. and Callahan, M. W. 2016. How Leaders Inspire: Cracking the Code. Bain & Company.

Centeredness is a core attribute	
Developing inner resources	Strong emotional intelligence including self-awareness, "in the moment" self-regulation, self-regard, agility
Setting the tone	Models integrity, ethical values, diversity, inclusion, openness, accountability, recognition
Connecting with others	Builds bonds, optimistic energy, empathy, mutuality, assertiveness, developer, expressiveness
Leading the team	Focus, vision, innovation, service, support, co-creation

In which areas do you already thrive in "inspirational leadership"?

Now using the attributes above, list 2-3 areas to put more energy into to raise your inspiration quotient. ______________________

____

Start by dropping uninspiring leader behaviors. While leaders can show up as inspirational using different approaches, there are a few common behaviors that are noted as uninspiring.[13]

[13] Modified from Zenger Folkman, Inspirational Leadership eBook 2022.

Exercise: Stop Being Uninspiring

Uninspiring leader behaviors	Add to my STOP DOING list (✓)
1. No personal development plan to grow yourself	
2. Encourages conflict, competing and comparison with other people and groups	
3. Rarely provides helpful performance feedback	
4. Does not share important information	
5. Lack of energy	
6. Tells others one thing, but does another	
7. Offers little direction and purpose for the work	
8. Never provides coaching, mentoring or supportive input	
9. Excessive pessimism and use of negative language	

Becoming more inspirational: You'll discover one of the results of becoming more masterful in the book's five keys is inspired staffers.

What is your top takeaway from this chapter? ________

____

This chapter addressed six areas for leading your unit: *Build your industry-related skills, make time to lead your people, lead with vision and strategy, manage change effectively, champion clarity, and build your inspiration quotient.*

The next chapter, also a part of the LEAD KEY, is a beginning investigation into what it means to lead your direct reports.

Chapter 3

Lead YOUR PEOPLE

Three areas for better team leadership:

1. Lead *each* direct report, as a unique contributor.
2. Reduce barriers to create conditions for individual success.
3. Build your team and culture development competencies.

Planning and implementing purposeful people development and team revitalization might be the most important work you need to do right now. That's because, even with great skill and effort, you simply cannot, by yourself, lead your unit (or the entire enterprise) to achieve its goals. Leading by closely micro-managing and doing everyone else's work is also ineffectual. (This happens sometimes with newer leaders who haven't built their team development skills.)

The way in which you lead each one and all of your direct reports has multiple effects that warrant your attention. For one, it sets the tone and cultural standards that will reverberate throughout the team. *What does your way of working and behaving say to your team members about the proper work practices, interaction patterns, and desired and acceptable norms?*

Keep in mind that each of your direct reports owns a piece of the work you are responsible for as the leader. How well each does their job determines the extent to which you achieve the goals set for your area. The work products of each direct report should be clearly and directly tied to your specific unit's results. So, leading a work group should look something like this alignment (though you may have more than four staffers). When done well the team's work results *should* add up to the expected results for the area you are leading.

However, what sometimes happens is: Even when talented individuals all do excellent work, it does not add up to exceptional results. The same four people, **working hard but at cross purposes** or in siloed ways, can look more like this:

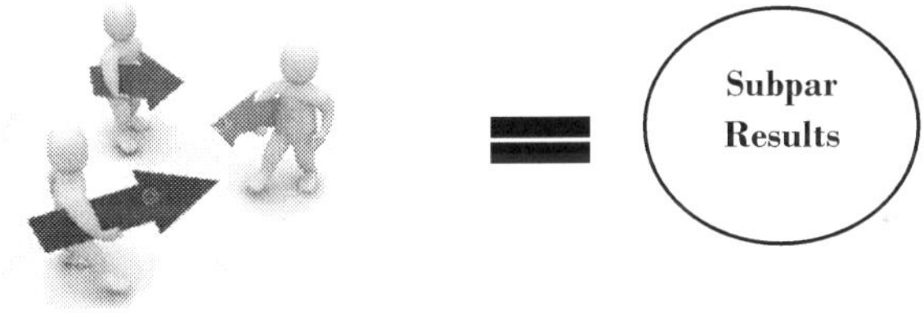

This can also occur when individual team members spend too much time doing good on low priority tasks and too little on high priority ones. It's your job as the leader to break this cycle and redirect each person towards the work that matters most.

Leading a high-performing work team requires skills for leading the individual as well as the collective team. A collection of talented team members doesn't *instinctively* translate to a great, healthy, high-performing team.

LEAD *EACH* DIRECT REPORT

Since four of the five keys addressed in this book relate directly to leading your direct reports, much attention on this intense work will be addressed in the sections called *Connect, Coach, Develop,* and *Perform*. Here, the emphasis is on you recognizing that one of your key roles is to lead each person as a unique contributor.

Leading *each* team member means figuring out what works best for each. How are you maximizing the potential of each? Forget the *copy and paste* approach, thinking what works for one works for all.

The highlighted black circle below is to remind you that *each* person is unique and brings their skills, strengths, goals, attributes, motivational patterns, and more that need individual attention to maximize their individual performance.

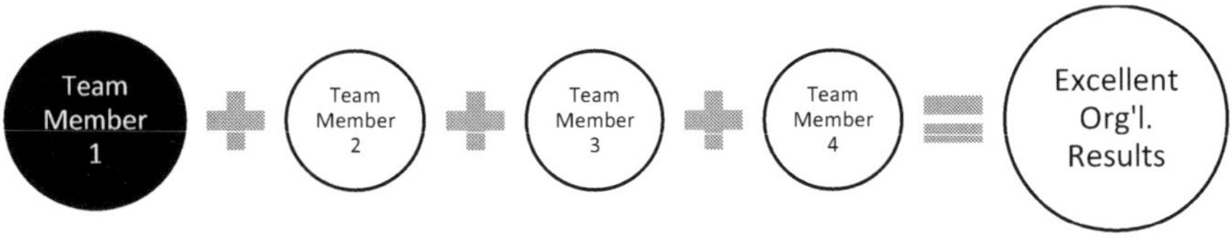

When you lead, engage, and develop each person, the collective results are increased, assuming you are also doing the work of healthy team culture building and maintenance (addressed in the next section of this chapter).

Don't neglect your high performers. Your star team members (those who are reliably productive and positive), who receive no attention are likely to get frustrated, feel undervalued, and deliver less than they can, or accept a job offer from another company. Retaining high performers is as big, or bigger priority, than retaining and developing average or low achievers.

In the case of disgruntled staffers, have you gotten to the root of their dissatisfaction? Some grumble incessantly if they believe they have no outlets to have their concerns addressed. Leaders, as reported widely, are often the cause of this disenchantment. Another person may be displeased because they feel they've been treated unfairly. There could be other reasons as well. Take time to think about what might be contributing to them becoming deflated complainers. (None of this precludes addressing issues such as toxicity and underperformance.) Avoid summarily dismissing the voices of your complainers; their venting may have some useful truths embedded.

Exercise: Improving Individual Engagement

The good news is that there are some things you can do to reduce these negative feelings and their drain on the environment.

Write the name of one "unhappy" direct report: ________________

To re-engage this staffer productively, place a check beside any of the six common ways to decrease dissatisfaction that you might try. [14]

1.	Motivate them more rather than harangue; try to instill in them that "they can" rather than can't.	☐
2.	Trust them more (with words and tasks).	☐
3.	Take interest in their growth.	☐

[14] Folkman, J. 1/7/2022., Are you creating disgruntled employees? zengerfolkman.com

4. Keep them informed. ☐
5. Be honest with them. ☐
6. Build better bonds and understanding of their needs, preferences, and talents. ☐

Now, enter the name of one of your high potentials and reliably high performing direct reports: ______________________________

Write notes on what you can do to develop and inspire them for longer-term growth, to avoid burnout, and ward off any feelings of under-appreciation:

Ask for staffers' feedback to help you lead each one better. Who would know better than the employee what might help them deliver their best work? One way to gather feedback is to periodically include a question or two during your one-on-one meetings, such as:

- In what ways am I helping you to achieve your goals? And in what ways can I make a change that will be helpful to you in your work?
- As the leader of the team, I want to spend my time doing what it takes to support the team in delivering their best work. So, please share with me: What should I continue doing? What should I stop doing? What should I start doing?

Annual planning for each staffer is another good strategy for a leader. Either before or following your year-end performance appraisal sessions, carve out time to plan how you will improve your support and development of each team member for the upcoming year. Here's a question format you can use, adapt, or shorten with each staffer (or have them draft responses to these questions beforehand, then bring them to the session):

Individual Annual Plan

Name:	**Job Role:**
1. What's currently working well to help you do your best work?	
2. What parts of the work are you most enthusiastic about?	
3. What contribution do you hope your work makes for the organization?	
4. Where do you tend to get stuck as you do your work?	
5. What support would help you do your best work (from me or elsewhere)?	
6. What 1-3 things would you like to accomplish this upcoming year that support our goals?	
7. What would make you even happier in your role?	
8. What would you like to see happen with your career over the next few years?	
9. How will you prepare (for #8)?	

REMOVE BARRIERS AND CREATE CONDITIONS FOR STAFF PERFORMANCE EXCELLENCE

When leading each person and the entire team, take note of the common factors that make it possible or nearly impossible for staffers to achieve their goals. Your job is to realign or get rid of performance detractors—that is, remove any barriers that interfere with each staffer's successful on-the-job performance.

One coaching client was deflated and ready to leave her job of five years because she had no time to focus on the actual job she cared about. The job description was great in her eyes but the frantic workplace that lacked good policies and processes caused her to spend lots of time solving individual problems— "firefighting." As she assessed the situation, she realized many of the issues could be addressed by removing barriers. That meant having clear and disseminated strategies, better job role coordination, relevant procedures to establish needed behavioral guardrails, and a guide for decision-making. One of her coaching goals was to coach up and help the CEO create systems and processes that addressed their chronic roadblocks. Additionally, she decided to say "No" more often to the fire fighting and direct more time to higher level goals.

Six Major Performance Environment Factors.

The example above illustrates how a deficient performance environment can defeat and deflate individual staffers. So, rather than consume your time micro-managing, spend it on optimizing the work environment to enable and empower your staff to do their jobs well. These words from author and coaching guru Alan Fine, emphasize the point:

"This person hadn't been performing poorly because she didn't know what to do; it was simply that there was too much interference getting in the way of her doing it! And sadly, the principal source of that interference was me." Alan Fine[15]

The six major factors, which either enable or detract from work performance (and which are largely in the leader's control), are:

1. *goal and role clarity*
2. *coaching and feedback*
3. *incentives and consequences*
4. *tools and resources*
5. *skills and knowledge development*
6. *effective selection/hiring processes*

```
Ask yourself: What might be
interfering with my team
members doing their best work?
Am I or my approach part of
that interference?
```

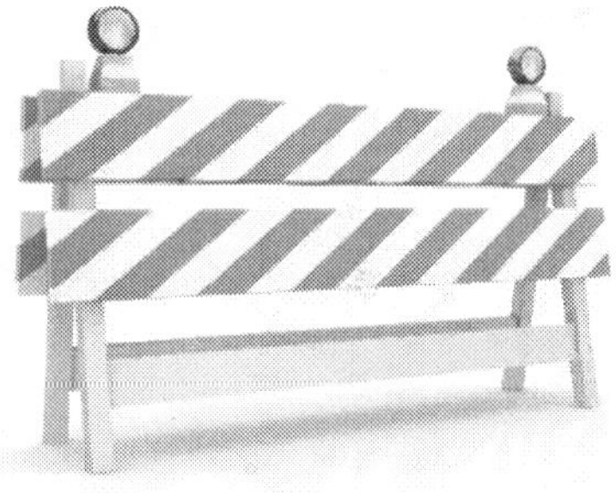

Ensure these performance factors are all in place. If not, clear away the barriers so staffers can successfully do their work. If you are facing performance issues with direct reports, try adjusting one or more of these because there's a strong likelihood they may be key causes of the less-than-expected performance.

---

[15] Fine, A. You Already Know How to Be Great. P. 12

Exercise: Questionnaire on Performance Factors (Place a check ✓ beside questions that you may need to think through.)

- □ Is each person clear on the goals, their role, and expectations for satisfactory performance?
- □ Is the performance process clear and fairly administered so people know how they will be evaluated, have regular checkpoints, and be provided support to perform well?
- □ Is the work adequately staffed with reasonable workloads and logical workflows?
- □ Are you providing one-on-one coaching, feedback, and reinforcement and at the right frequency?
- □ Does everyone have up-to-date tools, processes, resources, and appropriate space to do their jobs?
- □ Are there role models, mentors, or experts provided to show what the desired performance looks like?
- □ Are there the right and inspiring incentives for achieving the desired performance and consequences for less-than-optimal performance?
- □ Are direct reports provided opportunities and encouraged to learn and develop competencies for higher level work?
- □ Are all the aspects of and opportunities within the workplace equitable for everyone?

In summary, be sure you are keeping the workplace safe, inspiring, well-designed, and adequately resourced so your people can do their work, barrier free, at a high level.

BUILD YOUR TEAM DEVELOPMENT SKILLS

Team development (addressed more fully in Chapter 9) is a highly nuanced skill. Creating an effective team culture is essential to maximize your direct reports' talents and not fall into dysfunctionality.

There is no shortage of stories of a leader who is responsible for a set of high-talent individuals that underperform because they lack team cohesion. *What does that look like?* Observe your team to see the extent to which these are dominant characteristics: *competition, undermining, duplicating work, personality clashes, hoarding information, inability to collaborate, and more.*

Exercise: Quick team assessment

1. When you think about your direct reports as a collective, how would you describe them?

   ---

2. What have you observed about the team's functioning over the last 12 months that are points of pride?

   ---

3. What, if any, concerning interaction patterns have you seen among team members?

   ---

4. Have new people joined your team during the last six months? If so, what has been the effect on the team overall?

Developing a high-quality team culture and your team's ability to work together requires deliberate and ongoing attention. This is particularly true as priorities or team members change. Revisiting the common stages of team formation, such as forming, storming, and norming are necessary to achieve optimal performance.

A single person entering or exiting the team can disrupt or improve the persona and work relationships on a team.

***10 Attributes of leaders who are strong team developers*.** Since team building skills are learned, reflect on the following general attributes of leaders who are good at developing synergized, aligned, inspired, and high-achieving teams. These leaders:

1) **Model the behaviors they want to see in the team**. Think about your strengths and the limiting behaviors that challenge you. This kind of self-awareness helps you to lean into how you can serve as a role model of quality team behavior. For example, if you have a pattern of poor listening, or insistence on having your way, create reminders to keep these at bay.

2) **Build a team around objectives that will strengthen commitment to the organization and its values**. Guard

against building a cult of personality and loyalty to you. Diverse thinking and communication can foster innovative problem-solving. So, rally everyone around the goals and objectives.

3) **Set context** for everyone to understand their work and to do it in coordination with other team members, avoiding duplication of effort and ensuring effective workflows.

4) **Keep learning and observing what effective teams do,** the stages they go through, and how to sustain and develop them.

5) **Prioritize time for team development**. Don't make it an afterthought or something to do because it's on the calendar.

6) **Lead with positivity** about what can be accomplished, and find ways to engage each team member's talents.

7) **Are consistent and persistent**. Don't expect everyone to become warm, trusting, and productive overnight. Healthy teams require ongoing, incremental work. There will likely be setbacks along the way.

8) **Practice fairness, watching out for biases** by showing interest across the team, valuing diverse perspectives and styles.

9) **Build the team's conflict skills,** by fostering collaboration, building emotional intelligence, and better problem-solving.

10) As with the individual, **develop an annual plan** for where they want to take the team in terms of performance and culture.

The team's vital functions: As the leader of the team or workgroup, remain attentive to these three measures of team effectiveness[16].

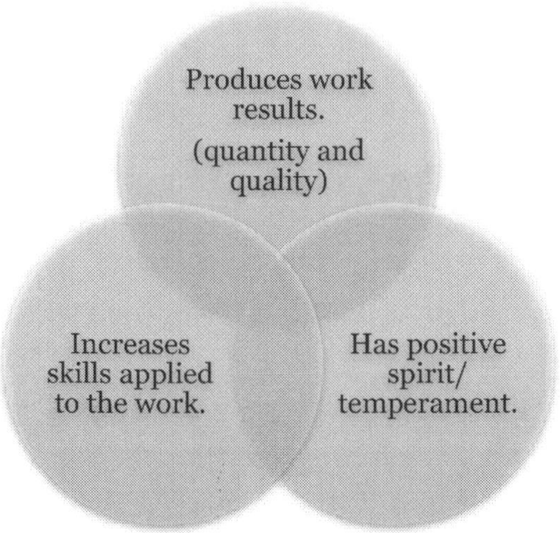

Exercise: Check In. Based on these measures of what a high-functioning team does and experiences, to what extent are these the expectations you have for the team?

Place a check in the box for those you feel are occurring now.

- □ We deliver both good quantity and quality work products.
- □ We are increasing staffers' skills that help get our work done.
- □ The team has an overall positive, supportive, collaborative temperament.

As you work to enhance your collective team, look closely at Chapter 9, which is fully dedicated to developing and sustaining team

[16] Peters, J. and Carr, C. High Performance Team Coaching. 2013.

capabilities. The tools and assessments will be helpful to both observe the current state of your team and to build a plan to enhance the team's shared outcomes.

Additionally, Chapter 9 offers signals for you to know when your team is moving towards an unhealthy state. Such teams will have less-than-optimal results, ranging from scattered efforts, duplication of work, redundant meeting topics, uninspired work products, etc.

Your team culture building work is ongoing, and having a highly attuned skillset is a differentiator. You are, at any given time, either a *culture creator* or *culture guardian* attending to the staff's overall work environment. You are creating a healthy, inspiring, supportive, and performance-driven culture. Or, as change occurs within the team's composition or due to shifts in organizational priorities, you are re-aligning the culture or guarding the existing one.

The state of the team's culture affects the extent to which workers *are attracted to the organization, want to stay, are satisfied, feel they are growing, and trust the leader.*

From here, spend time examining and planning for regular team development. That includes assessing, re-aligning, chartering, and team learning—addressed in the Develop Key, Chapter 9.

Exercise: Notes and Actions on Leading the Team

1. ***Continue Doing:*** Because these things I do have proven helpful to having a positive team culture and producing the required work results, I will continue them:

2. ***Stop Doing:*** What are a few specific items, related to how I lead my direct reports, I will place on my "Stop Doing" list?

3. ***Start Doing Practices:*** What are the 1-3 behaviors I will start practicing to strengthen my team development skills?

4. ***Post Practice:*** After two weeks of practice, describe how well you think you did on your Start Doing practices?

This closes the LEAD KEY which addressed sharpening your unit (or organization), self, and people leadership competencies. Now, we move on to the CONNECT KEY. All five keys work together to ensure your direct reports experience high satisfaction and deliver stellar work products.

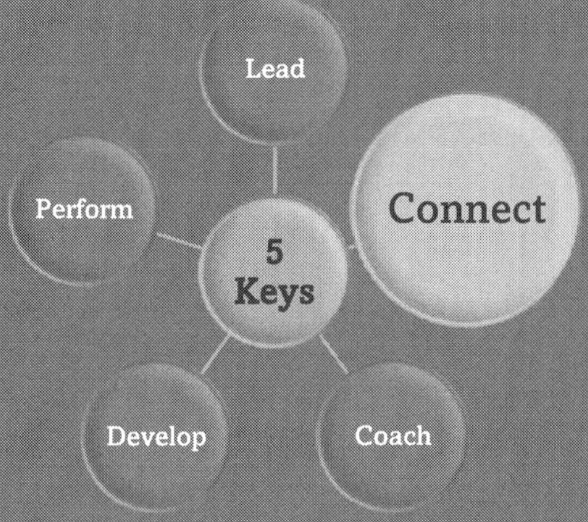

the CONNECT key

The "People Smart" Leader connects to staff through strong relational attributes, quality communication, and productive conflict skills.

The CONNECT Key: Enhance your relational aptitudes to achieve more with your staff.

Real Question: *I'm in charge. So, why do I have to figure out what makes each person tick for them to do their work willingly?*

The leader's ability to establish, nurture, and sustain mutually respectful CONNECTIONS with each staffer influences whether they do their best, average or lackluster work. It is one of a set of vital inputs for enhancing your people's productivity and for sustaining a healthy work culture.

There are still lots of leaders who view high relationality as nonessential. Some perceive amicable relationships with staff as an obstruction to engaging in job evaluative conversations, especially the hard ones. The truth is that connecting before correcting is helpful to achieve the results the corrective feedback intends.

Emotional distance from your direct reports is only purposeful in situations where you know that you will need to change the team's makeup soon. Even in that case, leaders fare better when they show respect and human caring towards all.

"The relationship between manager and employee represents a vital link in performance management." Gallup 2017

Chapters 4 and 5 delve into noteworthy factors and practice activities to elevate your relational savviness. Better connections encourage your direct reports to deliver their highest quality work.

Try this first. Connection Reflection Questions: Ask yourself these questions and if you don't yet have an answer, take steps to be able to respond in the future. Try some of the recommendations and reflections in Chapters 4 and 5 to create a path forward.

1. What do you do to intentionally build mutually satisfying work relationships with each of your people?
2. How well do you listen to your people with full presence?
3. Do you prefer your staff to do their work grudgingly or willingly?
4. Do you build a reasonably good connection with a staffer before you begin offering direct corrective (critical) feedback?
5. Do you generally display positive emotions, regulating any tendency towards negative ones?
6. Is it your habit to gather input from team members about their strengths, preferences, and needs?
7. Do you make yourself approachable, inviting input and sharing parts of your own story?
8. In what ways do you highlight or celebrate what's working well?
9. Do you demonstrate equitable treatment of all direct reports?
10. Do you show up with authenticity, concern, and integrity to encourage your staff to trust and be open with you?

Which of the questions do you need to think more about? Write the #s here: ______________________

Chapter 4

Better Connections with Relational Competence

Four areas for connections that yield better outcomes:

1. Relational competence a key for better work results.
2. It requires emotional intelligence and empathy.
3. Doable strategies to build meaningful connections.
4. Going too Far: Cautions, red flags, boundaries.

The ability to connect—to establish and maintain positive, trusting relationships with direct reports (and others)—is another skill that's singled out as a top leadership competency. Consider for a moment this statement from John Maxwell, leadership expert: ***Relational skills are the most important abilities in leadership."***[17]

Take a moment to imagine or call to mind (from your experience) what the absence of quality relationships between the leader and their direct reports can look like. Capture your thoughts:

---

[17] Maxwell, J. C. 2005. Developing the Leaders Around You: How to Help Others Reach Their Full Potential.

How might it feel to work for someone who only talks to you when there is a task to do or when they are dissatisfied with how you've completed a task? Many attest that it's not an enjoyable work life when you don't feel known, cared about, supported, and trusted. Think of your staffers—your recognition of their humanity matters.

RELATIONAL COMPETENCE IS KEY TO BETTER WORK RESULTS

Building bonds begins with acknowledging 1) a "strictly business" approach to leading your team to perform well is limiting; 2) this is not extraneous work nor is it pandering to individual whims, but a hallmark of emotionally mature leaders; and 3) people are not all motivated in the same ways, so positive connections allow you to learn what inspires each to excel at their jobs.

Relational competence is the ability to manage and engage in positive relationships with others and demonstrate it across people's diverse preferences and characteristics.

Ask yourself: How relationally competent am I? Circle one of the ratings below.

❶	❷	❸	❹	❺
Not very. Tasks drive me. People are messy.	Tasks nearly always supersedes people stuff	I'm Ok; not a huge priority	I'm good at this most of the time.	Connecting with all types is a strength

What are your thoughts about the value of relational skills as you go about leading your team? *(e.g., they are unnecessary, they are essential, they are uncomfortable and messy, make work better).*

Having positive bonds with your staffers (and colleagues) can yield better work results. Yet, some leaders are stuck in a dead or dying emotionally detached "I'm the boss" or "I only care about results" paradigm. They have not learned how to build bonds, or they haven't matured enough to know that establishing and sustaining positive connections with direct reports is an *input*, an *investment* in achieving work goals. **Balancing caring for your people's needs with driving for results will help you achieve better results.**

Connection story: *A leader's direct report, in responding to a 360-interview question that asked whether the leader "evokes trust among their direct reports" said "not really." Further they stated "He is cordial, somewhat friendly but he seems distant and detached. I don't really know him. I don't know if I can trust him." What followed were suggestions for him to reveal more of himself, what he really cares about at work, how he feels occasionally, simple nuggets about things happening with his family or hobbies (non-intrusive), and clearly show his "humanity" and caring about his staff.*

The leader-staffer relationship is a concern among several of my coaching clients and a roadblock for achieving quality results. I've heard leaders about a direct report who 1) is not adapting well to them as their leader, 2) doesn't seem to care much for their style, 3) won't reveal their thinking, 4) is disengaged and the leader doesn't know why, or 5) builds an underground dissenting coalition.

Such relationship challenges can make or break a leader. More than a few leaders fail in their roles because they didn't recognize or value the need to build effective connections with their direct reports. Unhappy staff can be the cause of a leader's undoing!

"Sometimes people attempt to hide behind roles– executive, parent, boss–they allow the power or authority of the role to replace the relationship. It won't work. Roles may provide the circumstances, but only the relationship can provide the foundation."[18]

Another way to think about relational competence is using David Brooks idea of *Illuminators and Diminishers*. His 2023 book, How to Know a Person, addresses building connections by behaving in ways that show interest in others as human beings. The challenge, the author shares, is that many people habitually draw attention back to themselves or spend their interactions broadcasting information rather than being curious about others. Thus, they don't get to know or become known by others. Here he contrasts the Illuminator and the Diminisher.

"Diminishers make people feel small and unseen. They see other people as things to be used...they are so involved with themselves that other people are just not on their radar screen...Illuminators have a persistent curiosity about other people. They know how to ask the right questions at the right time. They...make people feel bigger, deeper, respected, and lit up." pgs. 12-13.

While his book is relevant to relationships in general, it is worth asking ourselves: *Am I an Illuminator or a Diminisher for my team?*

---

[18] Flaherty, J. Coaching: Evoking Excellence in Others, 3rd Ed, 2010, pg. 47

Illuminators are curious and want to see other people in their fullness. They are curious. They can turn attention away from themselves and towards others. That's connection.

Which am I? My direct reports would most likely view me more like: Illuminator ☐ Diminisher ☐ Why did you make this choice?

____

____

Better work results: Relational competency shows up in better work results and a more satisfying work culture in several ways:

1. Leaders become aware of team members' unique attributes and interests that can be applied to enhance the work.
2. Employees feel known, valued, and supported.
3. Employees who have strong bonds with their leader (and co-workers) produce better work and stay with the company longer (retention).
4. Connected employees are more open to participate honestly and creatively in meetings.
5. People feel less anxiety during challenging times or missteps when they have a positive relationship with the leader.
6. Your feedback is received better, especially when it is challenging. Staffers know you have their interest in mind.

"The fact that employees perform better when they feel respected and cared for makes sense when you consider that company

culture has a much bigger influence on employee well-being than salary and benefits."[19]

> *I collaborated with a leader who initially spent half our coaching conversation convincing me that most of her direct reports were resisting her authority (three of four). She wanted me to "understand" she is right, and they are wrong. At first, she didn't own that she was not relationally very fluent. Once we stopped talking about <u>them</u> and turned attention to <u>her</u> ability to grow, she got on her way to more mature leadership. Though making changes to work on relationship building was somewhat uncomfortable, she was pleased to report, after a few months, she began seeing better work and attitudes among them.*

REQUISITES: EMPATHY AND EMOTIONAL INTELLIGENCE

Anyone in a leadership role should appreciate that empathy is a key aspect in managing workplace relationships capably. It has moved even further into the forefront since the Covid-19 pandemic shifted so much about the workplace, including increased anxiety and stress, adapting to new work arrangements, concern for workplace safety, and adjusting to radical changes in organizational strategies. These have increased the emphasis on wellness and quality of life. Revealing your humanity and showing empathy towards staff members supports, rather than undermines, work performance. E. I. guru Daniel Goleman offered these words:

---

[19] Seppälä, E. and McNichols, N.K. June 21, 2022. Harvard Business Review, The power of healthy work relationships.

"Empathy represents the foundation skill for all the social competencies important for work." Pg. 137[20]

Empathy, a facet of emotional intelligence, is to be compassionate and in tune with the circumstances, moods, and feelings of others—the ability to put yourself in another person's position. By taking a genuine interest in your team members' concerns, you deepen connection and trust with them. It helps you show up as an authentic person, and is known to reduce staffers' work stress, which allows them to be more focused on and invested in their work.

Advantages of leader empathy:

- People perceive you as a mature, desired leader who they will support and advocate for.
- Staffers sense you are engaged, rather than detached from their experience.
- Makes it easier to resolve problems and conflicts.
- Contributes to a healthier, more satisfying work culture.
- People, feeling valued, heard, and understood, do better work because they feel they matter.

People smart leaders recognize employees have lives outside of work which, no matter how hard they try, has a bearing upon their ability

[20] Working with Emotional Intelligence, 2011.

to do high quality work to greater or lesser degrees. At work, people may simultaneously be contending with a range of personal stressors. These may be related to family, childcare, health, aging parents, or social-emotional concerns based on their diverse attributes (race, gender, age, disability, and more).

Empathy, not to be confused with sympathy (to feel sorry), does not excuse low performance. It helps the leader grasp the staffer's situation, then collaborate with them to figure out how to alter work conditions to make it possible for them to contribute their best work and, if needed, find alternate ways to meet job expectations.

Empathy deficient leaders, on the other hand, are known to show up in these kinds of ways:

- ☐ Stereotype others.
- ☐ Show no understanding, misunderstand, or are surprised by others' feelings or actions.
- ☐ Often find themselves in the middle of conflicts.
- ☐ Cannot "read" people and what they are thinking and feeling.
- ☐ Tend to act without considering how others might feel.
- ☐ Come across to others as indifferent or uncaring.

Which, if any, of these statements resonate with you? ___________

____

What is an example, in your current situation, where empathy (taking an active interest in your team members' concerns) might be needed?

____

____

What you can do to display empathy:

- Really listen to others (without distraction) and tune in to their emotions around a situation.
- Set aside your perspective, judgements, and avoid defensive responses as you listen.
- Recognize and hold any style or preference biases at bay.
- Be curious and interested in each direct report.
- Allow staffers a voice in decision-making that affects them.
- Take action where possible related to staff concerns.

✓Which of the above (or other ways) can you demonstrate empathy without disregarding the need for work accountability?

____

____

Boost Your Overall Emotional Intelligence: There is easily accessible information on emotional intelligence. Developed by Daniel Goleman, he describes emotional intelligence/emotional quotient (E.I. or E.Q.) as the extent to which a person can *perceive, use, manage and handle their emotions and be attuned to others' emotions* IN THE MOMENT. I emphasized "in the moment" because that is a sign of the extent to which we have matured emotionally as leaders—when things are immediately happening. That is much better than allowing yourself to get emotionally overwrought, or as Goldman calls it, *hijacked,* during testy situations. In that case, the leader must then rebuild their credibility as a mature professional.

Goleman's four-quadrant E. I. model is illustrated here:

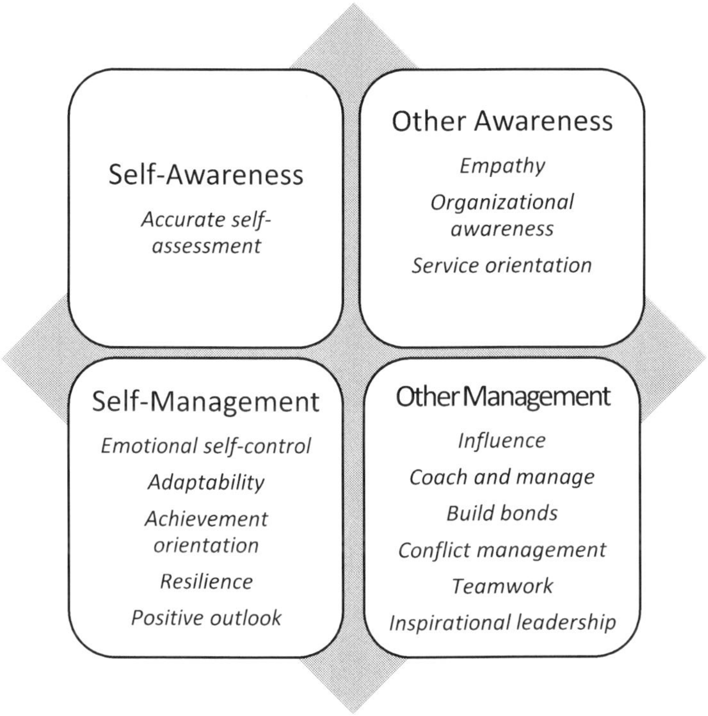

The model is a simple illustration of 1) our **awareness** of who we are along with our awareness of others and 2) **how we regulate and manage** ourselves individually and with others.

Exercise: Work on replacing behaviors on the left with the E.I. facets on the right. Circle any of your patterns from the left column.

Underdeveloped E.I. behaviors	**Strong E.I. competence**
Emotional outbursts—overblown and uncontrollable	Emotional self-control
Pattern of turning attention to yourself or your title..." I, I, I..."	Reorient yourself towards service to others

Always taking credit for successes, even others'	Improve service orientation
Emotions get in the way of working through challenges	Emotional self-control
Low empathy towards others (out of tune, poor timing)	Build empathy
Blaming others for your own problems; defensiveness	Increase self-awareness and resilience
Takes a lot to bounce back after challenges	Focus on resilience
Obliviousness to others' feelings	Build empathy
Overly self-critical	Build positive outlook/mindset
Poor interpersonal relationships, does not build rapport	Intentional strategies to build bonds
Difficulty reading the political landscape at work	Increase organizational awareness (recognize and leverage networks)
Need to be *right*	Improve influencing skills
Leads by giving orders, bossing	Enhance influencing and inspirational leadership
Inconsiderate of other views	Enhance teamwork competence, building bonds

Action: Ways I can enhance specific E.I. behaviors

Restate below not more than two behaviors from the left column that you want to work on to enhance your E.I. Then identify specific new behaviors that seem right for you. (*e.g., related to the first item in the chart, emotional outbursts- "I will take a breath and wait a few moments before responding."*)

Current low E.I. behavior	New behavior I can try

Specific E.I. blind spots were harming an incredibly talented senior leader whom I have coached. Here is a bit of that story:

A senior VP at a national organization, highly skilled at the role and generally upbeat, showed little regard for her reporting supervisor. She was convinced she was far smarter and more capable than he was. She made sure he knew it too, evident in her dismissive approach to his requests, her combativeness at other times, and unprofessional outbursts. What she did not realize was that politically this was self-sabotage. Her more senior leader was an introverted, slower paced, and perhaps more thoughtful person, who expected accountability and measured decision-making. None of these were in her domains of strength. She damaged trust and confidence. Her outbursts were additionally viewed as immature, reflecting poor leadership presence with him and among her colleagues. The coaching was to support her in rebuilding a meaningful, respectful relationship; that began with her showing regard for his talents and humanity and better regulating her emotions when she met with him and her colleagues.

Several E.I. elements needed her earnest, urgent attention. Which do you think?____

____

____

Unfortunately, by the time she turned to coaching, too many bridges had been burned and she was separated from the organization. Hopefully, she will apply her learning to her next work role.

DOABLE STRATEGIES FOR AUTHENTIC CONNECTIONS

There are a number of ways you can build positive, purposeful connections with your direct reports and others. Some of these ideas were noted earlier in this chapter. Repeating them will not hurt. These might be helpful in honing the skills of building bonds for both those who are not naturally predisposed to connect and those who are natural, at-ease connectors.

- Provide constructive, supportive feedback that encourages your people to develop new skills, correct unhelpful behaviors, and use their talents in new and better ways.

- Invest time and resources in activities that help you learn about each person's preferences, style, areas of passion, hobbies, and motivators. Use any from an array of instruments such as DISC, Myers-Briggs, StrengthsFinder, or Love Languages at Work. Extract what's valuable from this information to tailor your approach to each direct report.

- Show interest by asking and listening intently to your direct reports' thoughts, ideas, suggestions.
- Keep commitments on items you agreed to do on their behalf.
- Be present and available to your team members; make sure they can find you when needed.
- Stay attuned to, interested in, and as appropriate, responsive to what is going on in your staffers' lives.
- Offer assistance or pitch in when staff people need you, especially when they seem overworked, etc.
- In times of crisis, maintain effective communication, and model realistic optimism and emotional maturity.
- Show trustworthiness by modeling integrity. Do not throw your authority around with phrases like, "I'm your boss."
- Ask for team members' assistance, which shows you value their expertise and cannot do it all yourself.
- Reveal your story, what makes you tick, your path to the present and your interests; be human, not simply a title.
- Connect team members to each other. Help them answer: *Who is on the team? What is their story? What are each person's special talents, and contributions to the shared goals? How do we best work together?* (See more in Chapter 9, Develop the Team).

- Express positive regard and appreciation for what people are doing well and their value to the team.

Here is an example of what we don't want our people to feel or say (real story): *"If he's silent, I assume my work product was good. I only hear what's not working which makes me tense and affects my mental health."*

Learn about and **consider generational attributes and strengths**: One area that might influence an employee's style and how you build connections with them is the generation group to which that employee belongs. You may have allowed some of their characteristics to rub you the wrong way because they are so different from your own. But right now, there are four (or five) generations working alongside each other, and there is a lot of chatter about the differences between them. Though the generalities about preferences, habits, and beliefs do not neatly fit everyone, it is good for you to explore these attributes and build connections in ways that both honor these distinctions and learn how they can add even more value on your work team.

Exercise: Generations. Use this activity to see how and who might be showing up with unique generational characteristics.

The chart that follows is a general set of attributes, though not everyone exhibits them. So be careful not to typecast people based on them. Secondly, as you review the chart, think about how these characteristics can be beneficial to your team and its work.

Generation theme	General themes connected to them
Gen Z Born: 1995-2009 Change and flexibility	Clear direction and expectations, flexible work settings, social responsibility, diversity, recognition, wants mentoring, flexible, social, innovative, tech savvy, wants feedback and interaction, collaborative
Millennials/Gen Y Born: 1981-1994 Innovation and change, largest group in the workforce today	Clear expectations, seeks growth, meaningful work, relaxed environment/flexibility, results oriented, non-status quo, tech savvy, prefers coaching over "bossing"
Generation X Born: 1965-1980 Work/life balance	Entrepreneurial, relaxed environment, work-life balance, development, autonomy, efficiency, problem-solving, hands-off management
Baby Boomers Born: 1946-1964 Loyalty	Competitive, pride in work, hierarchical, approaching retirement, value chances to mentor
Traditionalists Born: 1928-1945 Hard work	Traditional values, formal structures, top-down management

Now, list your staffers' initials, generation, one way to build bonds with them, and one attribute to engage more or better at work.

Initials	Generation	To build better connections, I will...	One of their attributes I will engage better

GOING TOO FAR: CAUTIONS, RED FLAGS, BOUNDARIES

A new mid-level leader was having challenges with one of her inherited direct reports, who makes unprofessional comments, uses profanity when talking with her, chooses not to carry out her tasks as assigned, travels without authorization, and more. When she asked about the behaviors, the staffer said that's the way she talked to her last supervisor, who she said had no problem. Somewhere along the lines, this direct report was not held accountable for relationship boundaries, and it affected the new supervisor's ability to hold her accountable. She spent months setting up norms and boundaries for a healthier team culture. It wasn't easy and ultimately, that staffer was unable to adapt.

Boundaries: The best work connections between a leader and their direct reports are those where boundaries are clear and respected. ***Boundaries are guardrails between you and others that help keep the workplace wholesome, respectful, and productive***. It clarifies who you are at work as distinct from who you are with close friends and family members. Boundaries remind you of what's appropriate and what's not.

Quality and appropriate work relationships are not necessarily the same for everyone. The idea is to set up the type of boundaries that keep the workplace wholesome, equitable, and productive.

Some definite red flags: engaging in nonconsensual touching, name calling, using offensive language, sharing confidential information, oversharing, over-indulging during social events, showing favoritism towards work "friends," inability to give performance feedback to people you are especially fond of.

What are <u>your</u> work relationship boundaries?

What relationship boundaries help or hinder your team's ability to maintain a healthy, supportive, productive culture?

Help:

Hinder:

Better Boundaries Action: What is one "healthy boundary" practice you can either start or stop?

This chapter addressed the importance of the CONNECT KEY. Building positive relationships is not extraneous work; it is essential. The better connections, the better results, the easier it is to resolve conflicts, and the higher the retention. Positive connections matter with your supervisees and your other key stakeholders.

Chapter 5

Communicate Compellingly

Four interrelated areas for communicating that strengthen your work connections and get better work results:

1. 15 essential communication skills.
2. Consequential conversations require skillful dialogue, active presence, and deep listening.
3. Productive conflict skills go a long way.
4. Elevate interactions through assertiveness.

Establishing and maintaining positive connections is an important *input* into your team delivering their best work. An indispensable leadership competency, integral to these quality connections, is the ability to communicate compellingly and effectively.

Communication, as *a <u>two-way</u> process or system for sending and receiving messages,* is often overlooked. Each person engaged in or affected by a message plays a role; they bring their own thoughts, experiences, skills, beliefs, and attitudes into the message. Consequently, without work, many messages are lost in translation.

"We're not born knowing how to communicate effectively. Rather, great communication is a skill that nearly anyone can learn.[21]"

---

[21] Duhigg, C. How to become a supercommunicator at work. Hbr.com. 2/28/ 2024.

Skillfulness in this area entails communicating clearly, thoughtfully, honestly, humanely, impactfully, and with proper discretion. Conversely, low-quality communication is a major complaint in the workplace. Whether communicating goals, challenges, decisions, changes, or feedback, your manner, timing, quality, and clarity can make everyone's work life easier or frustrating and energy depleting.

One school leader known for blunt, harsh, critical language (viewed by her staff as insensitive, rude and belittling) asked me: "Why do I have to coddle adults and try to shape my words, so people don't get their feelings hurt?" From her vantage point, she considered these people soft or fragile. Very quickly, she found herself fighting against them as they joined forces to resist her authority as their new leader. The questions I asked her, as I suggested she begin rethinking and adapting her communication practices: What is your intention when you deliver messages in the way you do? Do you want to just be sure they know who's the boss, or do you want them to receive and act on your message? If it's the latter, then there's work to be done.

She learned, like many leaders, through missteps, that you can't walk around saying whatever you want, however you want, to whomever you want, or whenever you want. This entitled attitude will spell trouble eventually, first for your direct reports, then eventually you will feel the repercussions.

There are myriad signs that confirm quality communication is a differentiating strength. The best communicators: *get more done, have better work relationships, are more efficient, create clarity, attract people to them, inspire people to do more, demonstrate regard for people's humanity, listen well to respond appropriately, and thoughtfully deliver their written and verbal messages.*

Even the most brilliant leader blunders when "how" they convey message reduces the potency of "what" they are communicating.

15 ESSENTIAL COMMUNICATION SKILLS

Examining your communication habits will have an influence on how well your verbal, written or bodily messages achieve positive results. This sampling of essential communication skills (on the next page), when addressed, can strengthen your bonds with colleagues and staffers and help you present yourself as an organized, forward-focused leader.

Exercise: Try this. Think about your usual conversations, individual or group. Then, (on the next page), *place a checkmark (✓) beside the essential skills for which you currently have great strength.* Honor those, and then decide how you can use them in targeted ways to achieve your desired results.

After you have done that, *put a X next to just 1-3 where you want to make improvements* to become a more masterful communicator, using habits that help achieve great connections and work results.

Think about each statement as beginning with "I":

✓or X	
	1. ***Listen more than I talk*** to understand situations and others' perspectives, recognizing others have experiences that may lead them to view the world differently than I do.
	2. ***Communicate with candor*** being **clear and concise** about decisions, using a genuine tone and succinct, easy to understand statements to address issues.
	3. ***Reframe conversations*** to speak in more positive than negative (pessimistic) terms, intentionally seeking to reduce anxiety and to focus on what can be done.
	4. Maintain a perspective that ***keeps our shared mission front and center,*** steering clear of reacting personally.
	5. Give ***corrective feedback in the best, respectful way,*** at the right time and place with good intention for the recipient of the feedback.
	6. Give ***positive feedback publicly*** so other team members feel inspired and to give credit to others.
	7. Consider ***sufficiency of my communications***, being aware of what and how much needs to be communicated and what doesn't.
	8. Ensure ***I am fully present***, undistracted, so I hear and respond meaningfully to those with whom I am engaged.
	9. Use ***facial expressions*** that help people positively connect with me, rather than facial expressions showing displeasure or dismissiveness.
	10. Demonstrate inclusive communication by ***encouraging and integrating other and varied viewpoints*** and styles to improve my and the team's thinking.

	11. ***Paraphrase what I've heard (i.e., restate in my words) before I respond***, seeking clarity about the message a team member is sending me.
	12. ***Avoid impulsivity and defensiveness*** and give my brain time to process before passing judgment and when responding to feedback and conflict.
	13. ***Advocate for others*** who may be publicly disrespected, and support others' views that deserve to be upheld.
	14. Consider the ***appropriate channel*** for communicating messages (e.g., in person, email, texts, newsletters...)
	15. ***Practice transparency*** by being honest in what I disclose, clarifying my intentions and actions.

Further Reflection (related to the 15 items above):

a. I take pride in the skills I currently have related to item #s: ______________________________

b. I can benefit from making improvements related to item #s: ______________________________

c. Which items, if practiced, might help me manage conflict more productivity? ______________________________

Make a note to give more meaning as you go through this chapter: When I have communication breakdowns, they are usually related to: ______________________________

____

FROM TALKING TO *CONSEQUENTIAL* CONVERSATIONS

As leaders, we want to have consequential conversations with our staffers and colleagues; these are conversations that engage others meaningfully and lead to positive or necessary changes. They are not wasted words, time-sucking diatribes, nor insulting remarks.

For every important work conversation, ask yourself:

- *Why am I having this conversation?*
- *How do I want this conversation to go?*
- *What is the ideal outcome for me and any others involved?*
- *What change do I want it to help produce?* (in direction, thought process, mood, relationship, or knowledge, etc.?)
- *How will I manage myself so that I can bring my best to it?*

With time at a premium and recognizing your words have an impact on others, consider how to increase the effectiveness, influence, and inspiration that your words and tone carry when delivered and exchanged in conversation with others.

Substantive conversations involve *skillful dialogue, good presence, listening deeply, and advocating perspectives effectively.*

Skillful Dialogue: Less monologue, more dialogue

Some leaders have a predisposition to engage in one-way directive speeches when communicating with staff and others. This monologue habit (rather than an actual conversation) is everywhere.

For example, it is common for a leader to share with me a challenge they have with an employee. I inquire: So how did you manage that? They commence to tell me what they told their staffer. At some point, I usually ask: How did they respond? Did they understand the issue? Did they seem motivated to change? The leader goes silent; they hadn't sought a response. There was no dialogue. So, whatever the staffer thought or felt could only be assumed. "I tell them what I need from them," said the leader. This "just tell them" attitude is limiting.

To dialogue means there are two or more people in conversation. Dialogue, according to systems thinking scientist Peter Senge, is to engage "with each other." It is an exchange with attention to not just our own voice but equally and importantly, the voices of others.

Dialogue is more powerful and transformational than the monologue habit common among under-skilled leaders. The leader must be emotionally intelligent, curious and in pursuit of learning. Dialogue is never a war of words or attempts to win at any cost.

Good dialogue skills are the foundation of consequential communication, and these dialogue skills are prerequisites for other areas of leadership effectiveness, including:

- Coaching
- Dealing with conflict productively
- Providing quality feedback
- Effectively managing change

The next few pages on better presence and listening offer thoughts related to high quality dialogue.

Ask yourself: Where am I usually situated, during conversations, if there were a monologue-dialogue scale? ____________________

____

Better communication presence- physical and vocal

To be fully present with your staff members means not only being physically with them, but also *being focused, aware, undistracted by outside matters, and giving them your undivided attention.* When you are not present with your staffers, they can sense it and feel disconnected from you; they might assume you don't care very much.

When you are with people—undistracted and not preoccupied with your own thoughts, people feel heard, understood, and eventually develop trust with you. Your perceptions and intentions are conveyed with heart and purposefulness.

To be actively present, here are five things you can practice:

1. Find the right place free of external distractions.
2. Quiet yourself, breathe, focus on listening and staying calm. (A growing number of leaders are using mindfulness [structured practices to help with presence, attentiveness and full awareness] for this.)
3. Occasionally paraphrase what has been said before offering your opinion.
4. Avoid inclinations to multi-task (e.g., put e-devices away). Team members deserve all of you during their time with you.
5. Encourage the staffer to talk as you listen with interest.

What about voice presence? Related to assertive, powerful communication is voice presence. The voice affects others and the environment the leader creates. What message do you want your voice to convey? Does your tone and mood match that message? Is it the right quality for the specific situation you are facing?

Here's an example: A nonprofit CEO with 40 employees seemed to always project a depressing energy including low tone during our conversations. Inevitably, I'd ask how he felt at that moment. His usual reply: "I'm good." I couldn't tell. I wondered whether that was the voice he used most often at work. His "aha" was that he was likely infecting others with a downbeat mood, which was not helpful given the work challenges they faced. He practiced matching his words and tone, so the words "I'm good" resonated in his voice and helped improve the mood of his staff too.

Exercise: What is my voice conveying?

What signals are you sending through your verbal communication to and with others? Is it what you intend? Circle 3-4 expressions you believe describe what your usual voice quality conveys.

- ❍ Confidence/ assuredness
- ❍ Doubt in crisis
- ❍ Evokes trust
- ❍ Provokes fear/intimidation
- ❍ Hopefulness
- ❍ Gloom, dread, pessimism
- ❍ Caring
- ❍ Indifference or boredom
- ❍ Positive energy
- ❍ Dull or spastic energy
- ❍ Pace: leave breaks to invite others into the conversation
- ❍ Speeding train (no room for other views)
- ❍ Warmth/caring
- ❍ Other:______________

I worked with one leader who expressed herself when giving feedback in a child-like, sing-song voice, quite different from her regular voice. Another leader shared that he increased his volume and the heftiness of his voice when giving staff directives. Neither of their messages was landing as well as they hoped, so they paid attention to aligning the voice with the intent behind the words.

Practice: Pay attention to your voice so it conveys what you intend.

In what work situations do I need to be aware of my voice quality?

What will I do in those situations to project my voice in a way that matches my intent?

Deep listening goes a long way. Deep listening is an uncommon yet powerful skill. It helps you resolve issues faster and better, discover a wider range of possibilities for problem solving, expand beyond the bounds of your own thoughts, and overall, have more productive and meaningful conversations.

Six levels of listening.[22] (as described by Jack Zenger, leadership expert). Think about what level you are usually on and in what situations. (I have added Level 0 because it's also common.)

---

[22] Zenger, J. and Folkman, J. 7/14/2016. What Great Listeners Actually Do. HBR.

Level 0: The listener is just waiting to respond, distracted, overtalks the other person, and/or is defensive.

Level 1: The listener creates a safe environment in which difficult, complex, or emotional issues can be discussed.

Level 2: The listener clears away distractions like phones and laptops, focusing attention on the other person and making appropriate eye-contact.

Level 3: The listener seeks to understand the substance of what the other person is saying. They capture ideas, ask questions, and restate issues to confirm that their understanding is correct.

Level 4: The listener observes nonverbal cues, such as facial expressions, perspiration, respiration rates, gestures, posture, and other body language signals. Much of what we communicate comes from these signals. So, we listen with our eyes and ears.

Level 5: The listener increasingly understands the other person's emotions and feelings about the topic at hand and identifies and acknowledges them. The listener empathizes with and validates those feelings in a supportive, nonjudgmental way.

Level 6: The listener asks questions that clarify assumptions the other person holds and helps the other person to see the issue in a new light. This could include the listener injecting thoughts and ideas about the topic that could be useful to the other person. But good listeners never highjack the conversation so that they or their issues become the center of the discussion.

What's your next level and why did you choose that one?

____

____

Possessing basic listening skills means, at minimum, being physically present, quieting yourself to hear, and restating what is said before quickly offering a response.

Exercise: Better Listening.

Review these tips for better listening and mark a few as your developmental aspirations.

- ☑ Use positive body language, e.g., good eye contact, attentive posture, uncrossed arms, relaxed, nodding at times.
- ☑ Minimize distractions.
- ☑ Refrain from planning your response in your head.
- ☑ Talk less so you can listen more. Gradually cut the % of speaking time to grant it to your staff members.
- ☑ Reflect on what it feels like to simply "listen."
- ☑ Pay attention to messages that may be conveyed through the other person's tone and mood.
- ☑ Validate the other's thoughts as they share.
- ☑ Get comfortable with a bit of silence; it allows people time to process their thoughts.
- ☑ Ask meaningful questions, rather than always advising.
- ☑ Paraphrase to get clarity and show interest..." It sounds (or "I think I hear you saying") like you're saying..." "Is that right?"
- ☑ Keep yourself open to others' thoughts.

- ☑ Take mental note so you recall their stories, which shows you were listening.
- ☑ Refrain from interrupting or talking over the other person.
- ☑ Limit telling your similar story; let them have their time.

PRODUCTIVE CONFLICT SKILLS TAKE YOU A LONG WAY

I am not sure any of us are fully masterful communicators during conflict situations, but I know we can get increasingly better. So, growing our conflict competence can differentiate the low-credibility leader from one perceived as trusted and having integrity.

This begins with recognition that conflict is unavoidable and can also offer benefits. No matter how fulfilling a relationship may be, it is not likely that both parties agree on everything. Individuals have diverse ways of thinking and viewing situations. We also each have distinctive ways of responding to conflict situations. Our responses to conflict are influenced by our individual experiences, work hierarchies, the workplace culture at a given time, and more. You, however, can choose the best ways to engage in conflict to lead to better results. The goal is to become more skilled at managing conflict productively and constructively.

This statement from the book Resolving Conflicts at Work (K. Gloke and J. Goldsmith) makes a key point.

"Every conflict we face in life is rich with positive and negative potential. It can be a source of inspiration, enlightenment, learning, transformation, and growth or it can lead to rage, fear, shame,

entrapment, and resistance. The choice is not up to our opponents, but to us, and our willingness to face and work through them."

Conflict is natural, inevitable, and unavoidable if you think about it. If we assemble people with diverse abilities and experiences, we can expect divergent views. However, because many people are either *conflict averse or conflict bullies*, the advantages that can accrue from healthy interchanges can be missed.

Conflict is described as... *a difference or clash of perspectives or ideas that elicits strong emotions.*

Essential skills for effective conflict engagement. Because conflict management strategies may differ depending on the situation, being adaptable enough to try different approaches is crucial. Here are four skillsets for being a competent conflict engager.

- *Emotional Intelligence.* Demonstrate emotional self-awareness and self- regulation *in the moment.* Ask and answer: "What is happening with me right now and why? How can I regulate my emotional self to constructively engage in this conflict? How should I reset my attitude during this conflict?"

- *Empathy*: Ability to see things from others' perspectives. How can I engage in this conflict in a way that works for both parties?

- *Problem-solving:* To go through a mental process for addressing problems, then finding solutions that help those with different views cooperate and act upon agreements made.

- *Effective communication:* To use both verbal and body language to express thoughts clearly, help others feel heard, and ensure everyone knows exactly how they will move forward. (Review the topics already covered in this chapter.)

Reflect on your approach to conflict.

How would you describe yourself and your approach to conflict situations? What challenges typically arise because of this approach?

How I approach conflict situations:

These are the types of feelings that sometimes arise when I am in the midst of a conflict:

You can enter conflict conversations more effectively by:

- Shifting from being stuck on *who's right?* and *who's wrong?* to *what can we both gain from this conversation*?
- Recognizing competent people can see a situation from various perspectives; so, explore the possibility of seeing an issue in a new, different, or better light.
- Enter tough conversations by replacing your "absolute certainty" with curiosity. Ponder: "*What information do they have that I don't have? Is there something for me to learn from this conflict?* Instead of "*How can they be so stupid or illogical?*" consider, "*How might they be seeing the situation that makes their perspective make sense?*"

Take a moment to look over this conflict Thought/Action Flow. Each of the five items is explored below the graphic.

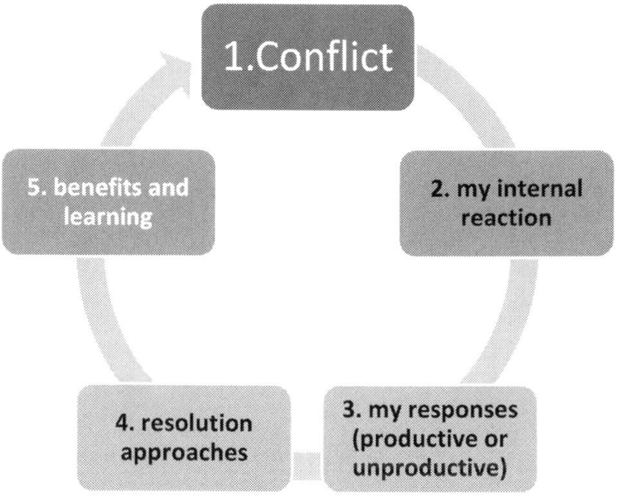

1. The Conflict: There are several common conflict types.

Four conflict types are described in a professional guide on conflict.[23] A combination of them can be at play at times.

Relationships personality or style clashes; feelings about how someone is being treated; interpersonal	**Task** lack of alignment on *what* the goal or task is, what's to be achieved
Process different views on *how* to get something done	**Status** disagreement over who's valued, in charge or gets credit and who's doesn't

[23] Gallo, A., 2017 Harvard Business Review, Guide to Dealing with Conflict.

I partnered with a client who sought to understand his challenges with a colleague. Based on the client's description, he decided the conflict was about process and relationships (communication style in particular). The client is process oriented and prefers a direct, efficient, get the job done approach rather than his co-workers' softer, "people sensitive" style. His colleague wanted to slow the process so people could give more input and suggestions.

His understanding of conflict types and the variance in their styles helped him go to his colleague with more openness. He shared his thoughts with her with words something like this:

Hello April, I wanted to talk with you about how we can work better together to complete this project we both co-own. Right now, it seems we have different ideas about what process we should use for communications about the next event. I know you are concerned about how people will receive our plans, and I hope we can find a middle ground that allows us to be sensitive to people while also following our agreed-upon processes. She was less defensive, and they co-created ideas that were better than each had by themselves.

Is the conflict worth addressing?

You always have a choice about whether and how to respond to a conflict situation. There are many advantages and learning that can come from engaging productively in conflict (identified later in this chapter). However, know your options for responding to conflict (as recommended in HBR's Guide to Dealing With Conflict, page 57).

They are summarized below. Reflect on what works best in any given situation. There are usually trade-offs with each.

Options	Best when...
1. **Do nothing**. Do not address, let it go, walk away.	You don't have the energy or time to invest in preparing; person likely unwilling to have constructive conversation; you have little or no power; it won't cause you stress or to beat yourself up about it; not that important.
2. **Indirectly address.** Circle around an issue by having someone else address it or talk about it without naming the incident (such as embedding in metaphors or stories).	Your workplace culture frowns on direct confrontation; the person might take the feedback better from someone else.
3. **Directly address.** Talk directly in the moment or at a better time.	You explain your view, listen well, remain open to other views, agree on resolution; useful when there might be lingering resentment unless you clear the air; doing nothing and the indirect option didn't work; desire to get a past positive relationship back on track, you genuinely want to learn and grow from it; it's a major barrier to work results or the work culture.
4. **Exit.** Get out of the situation entirely, last resort (leave job, supervisor, or project).	When dealing with someone from another department that you don't depend on for your work; when you have had enough and can easily find a new job; other options don't work and it's emotionally too hard.

2. **My internal reactions**: What happens within you when conflict arises? What are your automatic reactions to it? What meaning do you make of having to deal with differences in points of view? Some examples of internal thoughts that become triggers during conflict are:

- *They're trying to make me look bad.*
- *I don't want people to be upset.*
- *I'm going to show you I am smart.*
- *I need them to see they're not that smart.*
- *I'm not going to break down.*
- *I'm not taking the blame.*
- *Your ideas are not as good as mine.*
- *I have to regain the upper hand.*
- *It's not even worth acting like I care.*
- *This needs to end as soon as possible.*
- *They must not like me.*

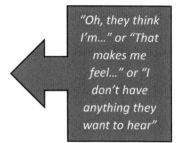

"Oh, they think I'm..." or "That makes me feel..." or "I don't have anything they want to hear"

Reflection: My common automatic *internal* thoughts during difficult conflicts sound something like these:

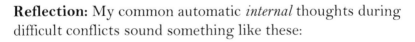

1.
2.
3.

3. My Responses. Exercise: When conflict goes wrong, what are your typical unproductive conflict patterns(s)?

Think of a few recent conflict situations. First, place ✓checkmarks in the circle beside the 1-3 behaviors of **others** that bother you most during conflict. Then ★star 1-3 behaviors that **you** display during conflict.

Arguing	○	○	Gossiping/complaining about someone
Belittling	○	○	Become hypercritical
Caving in	○	○	Overpowering
Defensiveness	○	○	Passive-aggression
Dismissing others' opinions	○	○	Revenge/trying to even the score
Becoming overly dramatic	○	○	Sabotage/introducing obstacles
Exaggerating the problem	○	○	Sarcasm
Exclusion/leaving people out	○	○	Being non-receptive/refusing to talk or cooperate
Blaming/ scapegoating	○	○	Withdrawing
Over-emotional	○	○	Ignores the person
Things simmer under the surface	○	○	Makes personal attacks

Summarize: During testy conflicts, my unproductive style is usually one of these: (from list above): 1)____________________ 2)____________________ or 3)____________________

4. Move forward: Exercise: Shift to productive conflict strategies.

Now, using the list below, mark how easy or difficult each productive conflict strategy is for you by placing either an ***E (easy), D (difficult) or OK*** in each box. Next, place✓ checkmark beside the three productive responses to conflict that might work best for you. Naming them can help you call on them during difficult conflict situations.

Apologizing	☐	☐	Finding a compromise
Determining root of the issue	☐	☐	Communicating openly and honestly
Stepping back to reflect	☐	☐	Separating your emotion from the facts
Owning your part of the situation	☐	☐	Showing flexibility
Giving people time and space	☐	☐	Revisiting unresolved issues calmly
Acknowledging others' feelings	☐	☐	Communicating respectfully
Seeking active resolution	☐	☐	Introspecting/being aware of your feelings & thought process
Giving reassurance	☐	☐	Listening

Are there any other productive ways you can respond during conflict?

____

____

5. **Benefits and learning.** Because conflict is normal and should be expected, spend time reframing your thinking around the benefits that might come out of managing conflict productively.

Benefits from conflict that were shared by groups and leaders:

- ✓ Helps bring out different, even better ideas (innovation)
- ✓ Creates interaction
- ✓ It can clear the air
- ✓ It can lead to resolution, move things forward, get unstuck
- ✓ Improves work relationships, better synergies as you get to know others' motivations, ideas, and talents
- ✓ Helps you better understand where people are coming from, what they value and are passionate about
- ✓ Could learn something new when you hear people out
- ✓ Reduces stress tied to lingering unresolved issues
- ✓ Demonstrates emotional maturity
- ✓ Others: add a few more...

We can only reap these benefits when we become more emotionally mature conflict managers. Effective conflict managers guard against allowing personalities and communication styles to take precedence over the real issue.

Exercise: Apply it. What is one conflict you had recently that you didn't manage well? If you could have a re-do, how would you resolve it in a way that honors both parties and gets to a better resolution? Think about attitude, positive intent, and productive strategies.

Name the conflict: (What and with whom?)

A better approach: (list new actions)

ELEVATE INTERACTIONS: ASSERTIVENESS

Boosting your assertiveness skill helps you express your views confidently and in ways that increase the chance of others being open to your messages. Assertiveness moves your interactions from time-wasting battles or quiet sulking to interactions that increase influence and decrease the time to results.

Undoubtedly, leaders will have views on a range of subjects, and these perspectives should be well-informed and *well-delivered* to come across credibly and lead to sound decision-making.

The book Own the Room[24] says that certain leaders (often introverts) are strong being supportive of others but weak in using their own distinctive voice—called Signature Voice or "voice of the self."

[24] Su, A. J. and Wilkins, M. M. 2023. Harvard Business Review Press.

On the other hand, leaders who are highly confident in their skills and expertise, can spend much of their time with others telling and sharing their knowledge as if it is the only view possible. While typically doing little listening, they end up over-advocating their views or aggressively pushing them.

Being savvy in *how* you assert or advocate your views while inviting others into the dialogue helps the team know who you are, what you stand for, and what your non-negotiables are.

> *"Leaders need to bring together two capabilities: – Voice for self: The ability to demonstrate your value and distinction – Voice for others: The ability to connect and align with your stakeholders."*[25]

Assertive communication not only gets to the heart of issues but also can help build authentic bonds. One of the conundrums I see with clients and perhaps all of us, is how to communicate thoughts, provide feedback, address challenges, and even offer compliments in an assertive way.

Here's a medical definition of assertiveness that I came across: *having the ability to express your needs and feelings clearly and firmly without disrespecting or undermining others*. Medically, it is seen as fostering healthy, prosocial communication.

Assertive communication helps the leader effectively advocate for themselves *and* others—receptive to other views believing they too

---

[25] Own the Room: Discover Your Signature Voice to Master Your Leadership Presence, p. 47

have merit. Assertive communication does not mean the other person has to agree or that you need to relent.

The lesson for leaders, who have not honed their voice presence, is that you don't have to let anger or frustration build up only to blurt out unproductive statements (usually with aggressive or passive-aggressive interactions, signs of low E.I.). Nor do you have to just "swallow" issues that need to be addressed.

Look at the graphic below showing four assertiveness stances, taken from the work of Randy J. Paterson, The Assertiveness Workbook.

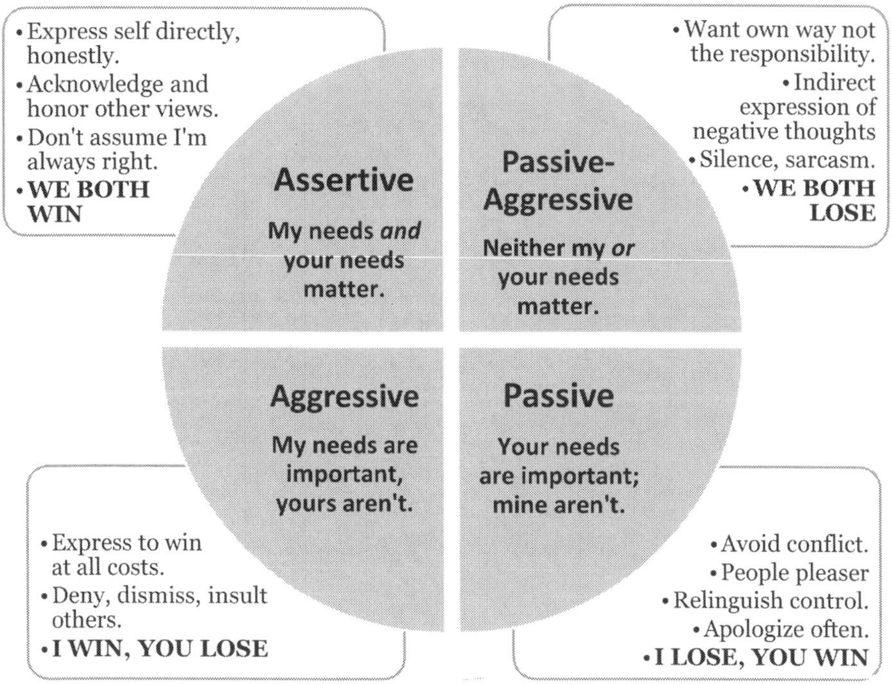

One top level educator comes to mind. She is working to bring her voice into leadership meetings to reduce her frustration and grudge holding tendencies. She is working on assertiveness and moving away from her default passive-aggressive style. She is reducing the emotional overtones in her direct interactions and limiting her use of sarcasm. After several months, she acknowledged feeling calmer, like a more polished leader, and that others were receptive when she expressed her thoughts. In essence, she is elevating her interactions.

Examples of various assertive communication stances:

- Internally: *I'm not going to say anything and just sit here.* (Passive-aggressive)
- *You did great on that, better than you used to.* (Passive-aggressive)
- *I'm the boss, and your job is to do as you're told.* (Aggressive)
- *Thanks for asking me, but that doesn't interest me.* (Assertive)
- *If you don't have your work done, just get out of my office.* (Aggressive)
- *Sure, I'm happy to come to the office (the morning after my birthday party) if you want.* (Passive or passive-aggressive)
- *Thanks for considering me for the project, but I will pass on that because I can't take on anything else right now.* (Assertive)
- *You're not so smart to me. In fact, your opinion on this shows you don't know very much.* (Aggressive)

To maintain positive connections and productive work outcomes, you can speak up confidently, take the stand you need to take, while leaving others' dignity intact.

Exercise: My Assertiveness Stance and Plan

1. Which assertiveness stance do you tend to take most often during conversations, meetings, or decision-making?

   ____

2. What's an assertive statement that might have made one recent situation better? ______________________________

   ____

   ____

3. How might you prepare for and express yourself assertively in an upcoming challenging situation?

   a. Describe the situation that would possibly go better if you communicated assertively: ______________________

      ____

      ____

   b. I will start doing: ______________________________

   c. I will continue doing: ___________________________

   d. I will stop doing: ______________________________

Practice this in your real interactions for more effective and powerful communication that maintains strong bonds and gets to work results.

Two closing connection stories

A change in view:

Marcus, a first time CEO, began our engagement frustrated about some of his board members. He set out to get a few of them off the board because he felt they were unsupportive, mostly critical, and not contributing much. A year later, he shared with me how great these same board members are, reminding me that somewhere along the line I had asked him about his relationship with them: Why are they on your board? What do they care about? Do they know what's expected? Have you spent time with them? These questions prompted him to schedule one-on-ones with them and he has come to experience each directly. He remarked about the difference relationship building can make to help remove limited views of people.

This made me wonder how many staffers risk losing their jobs because leaders have not built bonds with them to learn their motivators, talents, challenges, and needs. Maybe other leaders could try similar relationship building strategies, then rethink their view of and support for their more "difficult" staffers and their work performance.

Courageous conversation pays off for a conflict averse leader:

"It's taken some time, but I can say I am far more confident having courageous conversations with my direct reports. I have explored my fears about what I thought would happen

if I confronted the undesirable performance. I take time to prepare for the conversations. I also keep reminding myself that providing feedback is a way to help the staff person become aware of what's working and what's not, so they can decide to do better. I owe that to them. Additionally, I made space to hear their thoughts about my feedback. Amazingly, once I faced that part of being genuinely interested and supportive of this staffer, I became very comfortable sharing my thoughts and expectations. I hadn't realized that by having these courageous conversations, relationships can get better. To my surprise, the feedback is being well-received, and the staffer is doing better work."

This closes the Connect Key, chapters 4 and 5. This Key asks you to put in the effort to mature your capacity to trust, engage with, learn from, build bonds with, and honor the humanity of others, especially those in your charge.

We realize, even in our own experiences at work, people are more receptive when they have respectful exchanges with others, when they feel a strong connection with them, and when they believe they are highly regarded by the leader.

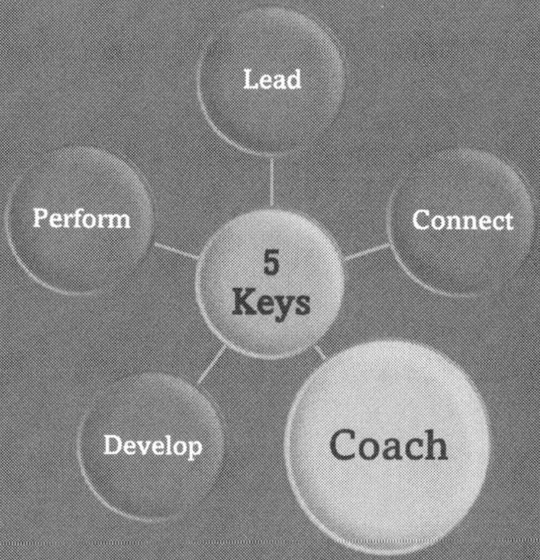

the COACH key

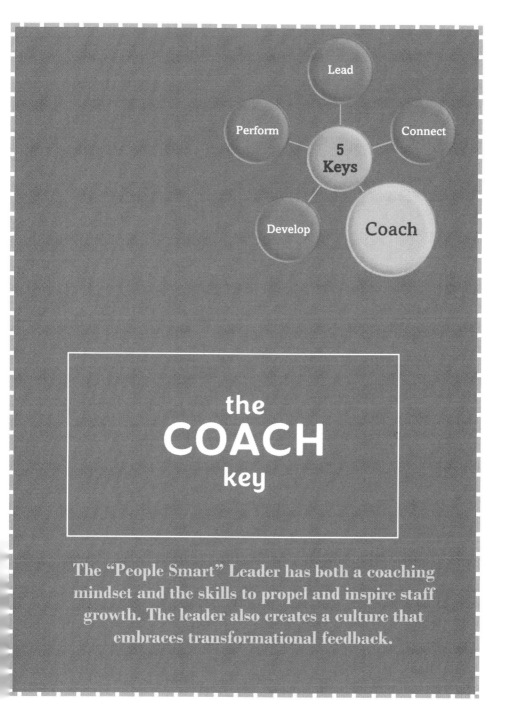

The "People Smart" Leader has both a coaching mindset and the skills to propel and inspire staff growth. The leader also creates a culture that embraces transformational feedback.

The COACH Key: Reduce Telling, Learn to Ask and Unlock People's Capacity for Self-Efficacy

Real Question: *Why are people so defensive when I tell them what to do? They know I'm their boss.*

When you release an "authoritative boss mentality," you can make space to embrace this mindset: *People will contribute more when they are encouraged and empowered to think, act, and generate solutions themselves.* This transformed mindset frees you to redirect more of your supervising time to coaching. Staffers will learn to self-assess, self-correct, trust their perceptions, improve problem solving, unearth inventive solutions, and build skills. (Some people find comfort with "bossing" because it doesn't challenge them to think and make decisions.)

Constant bossing hinders innovation, impairs problem solving, evokes fear and stress, and stifles motivation. Coaching empowers, inspires, improves results, and facilitates growth.

Establishing a coaching culture creates an environment that benefits the leader and their staff. Installing coaching as your primary means to develop, hold staff accountable, and build respectful, trusting relationships is a valuable addition to your People Smart toolkit.

Chapter 6 delves into the leader's mindset shift and a general coaching process for your staff's current and future high performance. **Chapter 7** illuminates the need for and power of quality feedback which relies on aspects of good coaching dialogue. Activities and reflections are included to foster giving and receiving transformational feedback. Let us continue.

Chapter 6

The Leader-as-Coach Mindset & Readiness

Four areas to prepare you for better leadership using a coaching style:

1. The mindset shifts for masterful coaching-leadership.
2. Consider staff receptivity to the manager-coach style.
3. Coaching as a mental model for accelerating staff growth.
4. Coaching, not a 100% solution; other methods are needed.

Let's start with a real story.

A leader, who was pretty adamant that "telling people what to do is my job," remarked: "If I don't tell them what to do, what makes me a good supervisor?" Over time, she learned through her staff's overt and quiet resistance and low motivation, that trying a coaching approach might come in handy at least part of the time. She began shifting her supervisory style (not completely because old habits are stubborn). One staffer who had considered leaving, having become miserable, reported, in a feedback session, feeling less stressed and more valued. She decided to remain with the organization, having sensed a positive shift in the relationship with her supervisor. (The leader, a year later, says she's made a lot of progress even as she continues to work on breaking free of her "boss" habits.)

If you aim to inspire your people to do their best work, exploring the Coach Key is imperative. Activating this key assumes you have begun building connections and increasing your communication aptitude with your staff team. (See the CONNECT KEY, chapters 4 and 5).

Those areas are important preconditions to ease your shift from a directive and autocratic style to one based on coaching your team members to achieve high performance. **Are you ready?**

Check in: *I'm ready to be good at supervisory coaching because I have:*

Yes__ Not quite__	Built good rapport with my direct reports.
Yes__ Not quite__	Gotten rather good at deeper listening.
Yes__ Not quite__	Established a habit of two-way conversation.
Yes__ Not quite__	Faced that "bossing" is no longer adequate.

Let's proceed. Using a *workplace coaching approach* to leading and developing your staff members will make your work easier and their performance better. A primary difference between workplace and external coaching (nonsupervisory) is that the leader at work is serving two roles: ***coaching*** to inspire and develop their people to perform and, at the same time, ***supervising*** them, which includes mandating and evaluating that performance. So, there is a balance.

Coaching at work is a series of development-focused conversations that enable and inspire direct reports to use their skills, insights and other capabilities to achieve in their work and personal lives with increasing effectiveness and fulfillment.

Here's another (paraphrased) description of the goal of coaching: Coaching helps our staff people *stop and question the thoughts and behaviors that limit their perspective so they can see a new way forward to achieve their desires.* Coaching helps staffers *who are stuck inside their stories and perceptions. Ultimately, it brightens their path* forward.[26]

THE MINDSET SHIFTS FOR QUALITY COACHING-LEADERSHIP

Because a sizable number of leaders are instinctively inclined towards "bossing," becoming a powerful coach-leader requires facing the need to *unfreeze* some common supervisory habits. Leaders must want to leave behind the frustrations and other challenges inherent in their pushing, prodding, and coercing before looking forward to the win-wins of developmental coaching. Consider these words:

"If people come to depend on you for answers, they lose motivation to think for themselves." [27]

---

[26] Reynolds, M. 2020. Coach the Person, not the Problem, p. 3

[27] Ibid. P. 24

***From*: Boss-Leader Style**	***To*: Coaching-Leader Style**
Leader takes on each direct report's challenges and responsibilities and becomes the hands-on leader of every situation, fostering dependency on the leader.	*Leader uses their position to uncover information about the processes, people, and culture that team members can use to resolve their issues. Staffers gain confidence in and use of their own resources.*
Realign Beliefs	
People cannot solve problems or create without your constant involvement.	Direct reports can devise approaches that work for them, rather than always adopting your solutions.
You must look over team members' shoulders because they are likely to blow it.	People are resourceful and capable of growth.
You are certain you would do a better job than team members, so you act in ways that create passivity.	Good enough solutions and actions by committed team members are developmental and will lead to even better results over time.
Change Behaviors	
You focus on team members' weaknesses.	You spend more time on team members' strengths.
You make all the decisions for team members.	You seek chances to invite team members to be decisive and articulate those decisions.
You assume more airtime than your staffers when you are with them. They learn more about you than about each other.	You invite team members to share ideas and collaborate with work mates to enhance work outcomes.
You spend more time speaking, making assumptions, and giving directions.	You spend more time observing, listening, asking clarifying questions, and inviting thinking and processing.
You assign blame.	You help staff accept responsibility.
You give the plan and tell your staff to follow it.	You support direct reports in developing or co-creating their plans.
You function as if work is life; all time is work time.	You bring a refreshed mind and body to work and encourage the same with staff, for the best impact at work.

There are all types of boss-leaders, so do not automatically assume you are not one. There are nice, micromanaging types, and there are the more extreme overbearing, arbitrary, high-handed, oppressive, even tyrannical types. The latter will have a tougher time making the shift and will need to be persistent in their efforts to experience the benefits of the coaching approach.

"Many managers are unfamiliar with or simply inept at coaching, particularly when it comes to giving ongoing performance feedback that motivates rather than creates fear or apathy."[28]

Exercise: Coaching Mindset Readiness

Review these prerequisites. Where do you stand on these factors?

Coaching readiness factors	rate 1-10 10, highest)
1. **Good listening and two-way conversation habit**: As you do more coaching in your one-on-one meetings, it can feel awkward being more silent than before. You may also become aware of just how much you were previously in the telling and monologue mode.	______
2. **Positive "people" beliefs**: The coaching leader holds a positive belief about the resourcefulness and potential of their direct reports to problem-solve. They do not always need leader-defined answers.	______
3. **No fear of loss of control**: Enhancing the performance of your people using coaching can feel like a loss of control because you are making room for others to	______

[28] Goleman, D. 2017. Leadership that gets results. P.47

	have a voice. Let go of the need to control every thought and action because it is constricting for you and your staff.	
4.	**Uses powerful questions regularly**. This will take practice and produce learning and connection. As you review the coaching method (later in chapter), take note of questions you can ask using your authentic, interested voice.	______
5.	**Open to diverse viewpoints**. Pay attention to any difficulty you have with embracing diverse thinking, values, and styles. Show you value perspectives that are different from your own as you problem solve with your staffers.	______
6.	**Prioritizes individual time:** Give ample, focused, and consistent time for your meetings with your direct reports. Remember, coaching doesn't necessarily take more time; it means bringing better quality to the time you spend.	______
7.	**Personally receptive to feedback:** In two-way coaching-style conversations, you may also receive feedback from your direct reports. Be open to it and resist any urge towards defensiveness or justifying your actions. Maintain rapport, composure, and good listening. And respond to the feedback thoughtfully or set aside a later time to address it.	______
8.	**Do not assume you are already great at it:** Some leaders say they "coach" their team when they are advising, cheerleading, mentoring, or telling. Many leaders think they are better than they are at workplace coaching, while staffers report otherwise. So, willingly explore this area of your leadership as though you are new to it.	______
9.	**Embraces four new(er) roles in your staff conversations**: The direct report is granted most of the talking time in coaching conversations, think 70% as a general gauge. Your time is spent at a higher cognitive level to make your talking more useful. Your four roles in a	______

coaching conversation are: 1) asking useful questions to stimulate your staff to reflect and think more expansively, 2) listening with full presence, 3) summarizing to ensure clarity and confirm next steps, and 4) sharing observations sparingly to help reframe and deepen their problem-solving.

10. **Uses good judgment:** The leader knows that coaching does not work for every situation. Inexperience can cause you to not apply it well or to try to apply it to every situation. Some situations require being more direct, more efficiency, or more urgency (addressed later in this chapter). ______

Make note: Which areas above, where you are already competent, can you apply as you begin leader-coaching?________________

____

____

"Leaders who ignore this style [coaching] are passing up on a powerful tool: its impact on climate and performance are markedly positive." Daniel Goleman[29]

CONSIDER STAFF RECEPTIVITY TO MANAGER COACHING

As you begin using a coaching-for-performance approach, consider the variations in styles and preferences among your direct reports. Most will feel relieved when the leader refrains from (or at least decreases) one-way directing and demanding and begins inquiring with questions like these:

[29] Leadership that gets results. 2017. P. 45

- ✓ What would be most useful to you in this conversation today?
- ✓ How do you think you can get even better the next time?
- ✓ What's another way you might think about that?
- ✓ What is currently getting in the way of performing this task?
- ✓ What support will help take your work to the next level?

Those, however, who may be so unaccustomed to having to *think* about how to solve their problems, so used to doing as they have been told, might be uneasy with this change initially. They may want to say: *"Just tell me what to do! Why all these questions?"* So, think about each staffers' readiness and level of receptivity to coaching's collaborative problem-solving interactions with you.

To increase staff readiness for supervisory coaching:

- Model coachability by showing your openness to receiving feedback, reevaluating your thought patterns, or sharing your current development areas. "To better manage my stress, I'm taking a mini course on mindfulness" or "I've got a mentor to shore up my budgeting and forecasting skills."
- Share your belief in their contributions and future growth, and your desire to learn from their views about the work.
- Let those who might be surprised by the change know that you will be shifting to a conversational, partnered approach during the one-on-one meetings.

- Be adaptable and patient if any of your staffers initially show low receptivity to you shifting toward more coaching and less directing. They may:
    - *Have little experience being asked to problem-solve.*
    - *Feel uncomfortable admitting what might have gone wrong with their work, i.e., worry about repercussions.*
    - *Not feel trusting or safe after experiencing you being judgmental towards them or others who have fallen short.*

The good news is that I have mostly seen staff being responsive to a coaching approach. Just remember, many are moving from *being told what to do* and how to think to this empowering, co-creating approach. This style values, rather than punishes, independent thinking; that is new for some, so be open and steady. Don't assume they are not coachable; try to uncover the cause of their reluctance.

Who is ready? Most people are. You can recognize your staffers who are more easily receptive if you think about **coachability characteristics**, such as these (they do not need all of them):

- ✓ expressed a desire to learn and grow.
- ✓ interested in self-improvement.
- ✓ seeks and is responsive to feedback as a way to keep growing.
- ✓ wants to be a partner in how their work is done.
- ✓ tendencies towards low defensiveness.
- ✓ usually good at follow-through.

I think about these factors when I am considering beginning a new coaching partnership with a potential client, to help us both discern whether it seems worth the investment of our resources. Or we agree to be ready for possible setbacks on the journey, since sometimes it takes a bit more time for a breakthrough in awareness to occur before the client recognizes the need and possibilities for growth.

Exercise: Where do you think each of your direct reports stands on being excited about you shifting to a coaching approach during one-on-ones, problem-solving, career planning, project feedback, etc.? Jot down brief notes on how to ensure their or your readiness.

Direct Report	**View of receptivity**

Hopefully, you will recognize most, or all are ready, especially if you are. Next, let's look at a workplace coaching process.

COACHING MENTAL MODEL FOR ACCELERATING GROWTH

The premise of coaching is that people generally can discover, for themselves, the solutions they need and that are suitable for them. The role of the coach-supervisor then becomes to provide guidance and a supportive framework to do so.

Internalize this graphic (on the next page) or simplify it to make it more memorable for you. Turn it around in your mind.

View it as a general, adaptable process. It should never be a rigid, rote process. Over time, like brushing your teeth, you will not need someone to say: 1) pick up the brush, 2) add toothpaste, 3) place the brush on your teeth and 4) brush for 30 seconds at the top and 30 at the bottom. It will become natural.

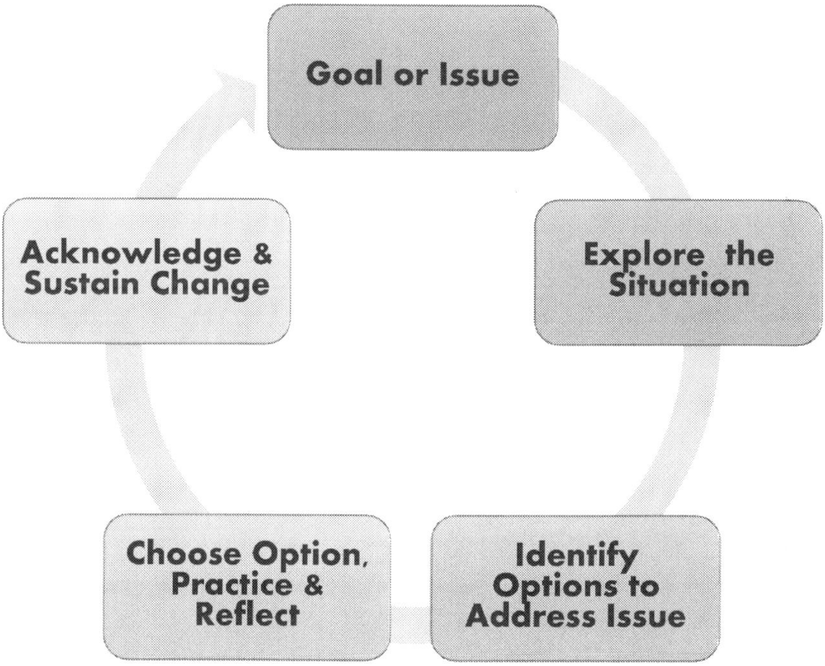

Since there are many paths to arrive at the needed results, use coaching to allow your staffers to choose theirs (within your workplace's established parameters). People are more likely to act on ideas they generated or at least helped to generate.

Listen more, talk less: During coaching conversations, the speaking time largely belongs to the staffer. They are given time and space for *thinking, reflecting, reframing, problem-solving, questioning and evaluating their assumptions, and more*. Your job is to create the setting for them to do so by *asking useful questions to help them reflect; listening; summarizing; or sharing observations sparingly.*

Here is a contrast between a directive and coaching conversation.

Directive focus on performance (mostly leader-centered monologue)	**Coaching for performance** (mostly staffer-centered dialogue)
***Leader**: Let's look at your work projects from last month. It seems you are doing well on Project X and falling short on Project Y. As I observed you, you are spending too much time on the project you enjoy most, X, and not enough on Project Y. This shortfall can come back to haunt you at evaluation time. There are several things you need to do. You need to be a better time manager, delegate some tasks to your colleagues, stop taking long lunches, and do better thinking about how the project will succeed. I also noticed this is the third*	***Leader**: Are you ready to share your thoughts on your work projects from last month?* ***Staffer**: Sure.* ***Leader**: Why not walk through what's most important about them? I look forward to hearing your thoughts.* ***Staffer**: I've done well on Project X and clients are receiving it well. The team is working well on it. Regarding Project Y, I feel we can do a lot better once I figure out how to get more team members on board and secure the technology we need to communicate and execute the tasks more efficiently. With many of the team members working remotely, having tech issues slows things down. Overall, I think we can get there over the next few months.*

month you've fallen short. That's disappointing. Ok, are we clear on what you will do next to meet your goals? ***Staffer***: *Yes, but I don't think the way you described the challenges are accurate.* ***Leader***: *Well, that's what I see, and I need you to address what I just laid out. Let's talk again next week.*	***Leader***: *For clarity, what are your thoughts on what to do to get Project Y on track?* ***Staffer***: *I will work closely with IT this week to shore up the project management system. I am also having meetings with the two staffers who are not fully bought in. I'm sure it's because they don't understand what their roles are and what to prioritize. That will get us going. I'll give them more clarity.* ***Leader***: *So, you're confident you will be able to complete these projects successfully before next month's deadline?* ***Staffer***: *No doubt about it. These are great projects, we have the skills and motivation, just a few adjustments, and you can count on us to get it done.* ***Leader***: *Anything you need from me to support your work?* ***Staffer***: *I think we're good, except I need your confidence that I can get the project done. And I will. So, a positive nudge now and then works.*

What differences do you see in the two examples? ______________

____

____

What insight did you receive after reading these two examples?

____

____

Exercise: Practice the coaching approach

This is a chance to practice putting the coaching process into action. Modify the questions to fit your natural style and language. Coaching should not be robotic; it should feel like a normal conversation.

1. Select a direct report, friend, or colleague who has a current goal or opportunity they'd like to pursue or achieve.
2. Ask them to allow you to walk them through a coaching conversation to see where and how it goes.

You will not need all the questions included on the worksheet, so decide which ones work best. Additionally, you may get answers to some questions when the person is responding to another, so be flexible. **Asterisks are some questions that matter most.**

GOAL- Here you are trying to get clear on the purpose of the conversation. This clarity creates the focus and direction for the conversation. Ultimately, you are coaching to develop and grow the staff, to move them to new levels of competence.

What topic or situation do you want to address and resolve? * (Paraphrase to confirm clarity)	
Why is that important? *	

What might happen if you don't address it?	

EXPLORE the situation- You are trying to get a sense of what is happening, why it matters, and what's keeping the problem in place.

What's been happening with this issue? *	
What have you already tried? *	
What are the obstacles to getting this resolved?	
What role might you be playing in not getting this resolved?	

OPTIONS- This is an empowering element, with the purpose here being to allow the staffer to think through what they have already done, what they can do, what is already helping, and which options would be next and the best ways to address the issue identified in the goal.

Can you think of a few ways you can resolve the issue? * Don't block any ideas.... What else?	
What might someone watching this situation recommend?	
What if you took an entirely fresh approach?	
Would you like suggestions from me?	
Which options sound like the best way forward? *	

ACTIONS (Where next?)- Here is where the conversation moves from talking and thinking to real-world committed action. How is the person being coached agreeing to move forward (actions) and by when? Is there confidence and commitment to do so?

For clarity, what actions/options will you take next to address this issue? *	
When will you do this?	
What do you need to keep yourself accountable for doing this? Do you need anything from me?	
How will you address any obstacle that might get in the way?	

ACKNOWLEDGE & REPORT BACK –this is the accountability part of coaching where the staffer, after the agreed upon time, shares the results of their actions, their feelings and learning about their actions, and how to continue working on the goal so new learning and habits are developed.

After the agreed upon time (for follow up on actions) ... What worked? * What didn't?* What did you learn in the situation? How can you do more of what worked? * What can you do to sustain the change you've made?	

Reflection: How did this practice coaching conversation go? What worked well? What would you change? Write some notes here.

Workplace coaching can be used in several ways, such as:

- On the spot coaching (quick, taking only a few minutes).
- One-on-one meetings for 45-60 minutes at regularly scheduled times (see sample format at end of this chapter.)
- Career development: "I want to grow my career here at our organization. What do you suggest?" (Work through the process.)
- Review of tasks or projects. Use the coaching approach to garner staffers' thoughts on their work and how to move forward.

Two examples:

- A staffer comes to you and says, "I have no idea how to deal with my colleague. His behavior frustrates me." A quick coaching engagement might go like this (always ask one question at a time and give time for a response): *What makes it frustrating? What have you done to try to collaborate better with him? What is one thing you can try to initiate a better style of relating? Any other ideas? Go try it and see how it goes, and let's check back in after your meeting with him.*

- A staffer coordinated a parent's meeting that went better than ever. You might first affirm them for their success. Then: *The event was excellent. What did you do differently as you lead it this year? What parts really seemed to have had the most positive impact on the parents? What would you keep for the next time? I suggest you document it, so next year you can build on it or help ensure it is as well executed as this year. Good job!*

With a developmental coaching supervisory approach, people grow quicker to new levels of competence and confidence. One leader, after a few years of applying supervisory coaching with staff, remarked:

"One benefit of coaching is that when staff learn to problem solve and not rely on the leader to solve every problem, time is freed up to do what the leader is passionate about and responsible for at a higher level and with greater focus."

WHEN COACHING IS NOT THE RIGHT CONVERSATION

Coaching works! Coaching works! Yet, there are still times when staffers need other types of interactions with the supervising leader. These might range from being direct, giving advice, to teaching a specific process or skill. Use good judgment, and don't waste time trying to coach around a topic that cannot be resolved by coaching.

Directing. Be direct and straight forward when people are, for example, learning a new skill, something is fully outside of their repertoire, when time is limited, or work products haven't improved using coaching. If there is a process for something that the staffer is not familiar with, just tell them. When there is a specific way results must be achieved, coaching will not bring the clarity needed. If there are not any options, just tell people how something is to be done or what they must do (no need to keep going back and forth). And if something needs to take place immediately, say it: "I need you to do this task tomorrow morning. We can debrief later."

Advising: This is to offer *your* ideas on how to best do something, and in *a few instances*, it makes sense. Leaders should be aware that what makes advice-giving problematic is that you are often saying what works for you. However, what works for one person is not necessarily the best way forward for another.

Advice can be helpful when there is an entirely new situation, a staffer has no experience to draw from, or when you're asked for your advice. In the latter case, provide one or two examples of how things have been approached, then leave it to them to explore whether any might be suitable. Sometimes, when coaching, a staffer can get stuck; here you may ask to offer advice, then give them room to take it or not.

Teaching: Coaching doesn't help when people need more skills. It won't do much good to ask someone what they think is the best way to do brain surgery; aptitude requires more direct learning. If a person really needs to learn about time management, provide skill building options. There are definitely instances when structured teaching and learning are necessary.

Closing Reflection*:* Recall a recent meeting with a direct report. To what extent did you show up as a coaching leader using these four roles? Write a rating in the space on the graphic using 1 - 5 (with 5 as the highest).

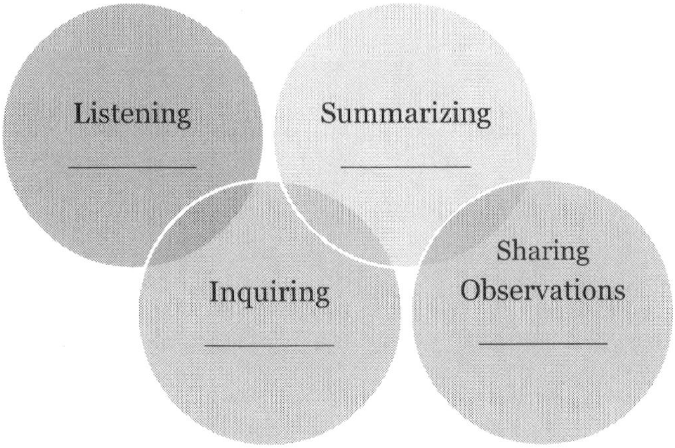

1. What percentage of the time do you estimate YOU were talking? _____ (if more than about 30%, adjust.)
2. Was your direct report able to get to some actionable solutions to which they could commit? _____________

(Keep these roles in mind for coaching situations. Other times, as a leader, you will play a different role with other suitable practices.)

The Coach Key in Chapter 6 addressed how to have coaching conversations to accelerate direct reports' growth and learning, build problem-solving skills, and create a more fulfilling workplace.

Giving useful, quality feedback is also a major growth area for leaders. So, on to Chapter 7 which is a part of The Coach Key section because giving and receiving value-adding feedback is a form of coaching that is essential to higher performance.

Sample One-on-one Coaching Meeting Guide

Here is an example of an adaptable coaching-style meeting with each direct report. It is best for 45–60-minute meetings. This allows you to partner with your staff to look back and forward—including relevant updates, problem-solving, and future plans.

Minutes	The Flow (flexible)	Purpose
3	How are things?	A moment to connect with direct report's current state before shifting topics.
5	What's been going well since our last conversation?	To learn of and affirm what's working well in their work
3	What's the most important things we should talk about today?	The direct report's agenda and priority topics (to address during this session)
10	Can you check in on the actions you agreed to take the last time we talked?	To check accountability for anything the direct report committed to do during your last meeting
15	How about looking at the topics you have?	This allows direct report to have your ear and support as they address pressing work or career issues.
10	Any project/work updates to share?	This should cover perceptions of performance.
3	What will you do specifically to move forward?	These are the direct reports action steps in response to goals and challenges they are pursuing in their work

5	Closing: Updates and support. Are there things you'd like from me to support you as you move forward? I have a few quick updates before we end.	This shows the partnership role you play with your direct reports. You can also suggest a way to support and check if that would be useful to them. Share few quick updates or reminders.

Chapter 7

Great Feedback Goes A Long Way

Three topics for skillful, transformational feedback:

1. Feedback is a powerful lever to advance the work.
2. Feedback anxiety—overcome it for the sake of your people.
3. Give feedback people can use: A method and when to use it.

This is probably a more crucial skill requirement than you might think. At least half of the leaders I have worked with required some attention to getting better with feedback to make progress on their goals. Several talked of being stumped about how to address a challenge with a staffer, colleague, or their leader. Eventually, I ask: *Have you shared the issue with them? Did you deliver it in the best way? Were you receptive to their feedback as well?*

Similar to overcoming anxieties related to managing conflict, these leaders focused on giving, receiving, and expecting beneficial results from feedback. As they improved their feedback practices, they described their troubling relationships and performance improving.

We owe it to our people to offer quality feedback; but many of us avoid it, and our people dread it, having learned to fear it. That's because most of us are not particularly good at it, but we can be.

Feedback, closely related to *coaching*, has its own chapter because:

- It is a foundational skill that many leaders need to get more comfortable with and better at.
- There is not enough of it going around, and *everyone* needs and can benefit from regular, well-executed feedback.
- People tend to think mostly of its "corrective" form, though "affirming" feedback is much better for inspiring growth.

To make a subtle distinction, coaching is seen as developmental and *forward-looking*, while feedback reflects on *past behaviors*.

Gallup reported that *only* 26% of employees rate their managers' feedback as helpful to how they do their work.[30]

Is most of your feedback to staff affirming and reinforcing? Yes ___ No______. It should be.

Feedback is information. At work, when delivered effectively, it is *contributory* information that our staffers need to hear to enhance their work, skills, and behaviors. **There are two types**:

1. *affirming* (positive, reinforcing, confirming what's working).
2. *corrective* (to address missteps for better future actions).

To deliver it well, use the coaching skills of clarifying the goal, two-way dialogue, inquiry, exploring alternatives, and attentive listening.

FEEDBACK, A POWERFUL LEVER FOR GROWTH

Feedback, offered regularly and with good intent, facilitates and accelerates learning and positive change. It helps our staffers see things they might not see (blind spots), including positive attributes.

---

[30] Wigert, B. and Dvorak, N., Feedback is not enough, gallup.com, May 16, 2019

They can become aware of and receive reinforcement for doing well on specific tasks or relationships, or they can gain insight into how they may have veered off track, missed a target or a critical step.

Look at these instances where value-adding feedback might have helped the employee better direct their efforts:

- ✓ A staffer works super hard only to discover, after expending enormous amounts of energy, the leader had expected them to spend their time on other tasks. Withholding feedback can lead to frustration: *"Wow, if I had known, I would have done the other tasks rather than keep working the same way."*
- ✓ Employees have been tasked to do things for which they have not been trained or mentored, but they do their best only to hear they messed it up. Providing instruction and feedback along the way could have helped them.
- ✓ An employee did a stellar job on their project and never heard that their work outputs were exceptional and valued. This can have the effect of the employee not repeating those tasks believing they might not have been that important.
- ✓ A staffer gets frustrated and makes rude outbursts that undermine their public credibility. Without feedback to correct this pattern, they might continue self-sabotaging.

Team members <u>need</u> and <u>want</u> to know whether they are making progress or just going through the motions. They want to use their talents in the best way and correct patterns as they go. Feedback is a *contributory leader skill* in such cases. Helpful feedback is transformational, directional, even inspirational. A feedback-rich culture is a place in which people perceive they and their work are valued, supported, connected, and purposeful.

OVERCOME FEEDBACK ANXIETY

A first step in getting good at providing quality feedback is having the right mindset about its value. Many leaders suffer from *feedback avoidance* or have underdeveloped feedback muscles.

Beliefs about feedback (along with lack of skill) often play a role in this avoidance and anxiety. You may have residual feelings from times feedback you received or gave did not yield good results. Or you might anticipate people will react poorly to critical comments. (There are times when people will react emotionally since they may view it as overly critical and damaging to their self-worth. They and you get through it when you manage it with good intent and delivery.)

Our feedback anxieties and beliefs can cause us to wait to provide it until things have gotten so bad that we feel— "I can't take it anymore." Others think positive feedback is unnecessary, believing a paycheck should be sufficient. Or you wait until a list of infractions builds up to make you bold enough and justified in providing it. Then others, afraid of the recipient's possible response, overtalk or over explain it to the point the feedback is obscured and useless. None are good practices, since these make it likely that the feedback is carelessly planned and does not land well.

Exercise: Feedback beliefs and intention. Explore your thoughts about giving and receiving feedback.

1. How receptive are you to receiving, even encouraging, others to offer you feedback? (whether positive or corrective)?

2. What beliefs may be keeping you from giving *positive* feedback?

3. What attitude might be holding you back from giving more *corrective* feedback?

4. What, generally, are your intentions when giving feedback?

5. What is a recent situation in which you wanted to give better, more useful feedback?

6. Practice: Think about the situation in question 5. Now write how you might have provided it more effectively.

Think about micromanaging Janet, who does her next level leader's work, saying she can't trust him, as a manager, to do his work the way she wants it done. When I asked, Janet answered No to these questions: *Does Darryl know why you are doing his work and working with his supervisees? Does he know what he needs to do or produce to fulfill the job needs and allay your anxieties?* Janet and I then talked about the value of feedback, how without it, she is doing a disservice to Darryl, his team members and herself (through overwork). She began offering better feedback and saw progress and ownership in Darryl's work. She also regained time to focus on her own work.

Your receptivity to it makes you a better feedback giver. Creating a feedback-appreciative workplace happens when leaders model that personal growth is important and can happen through quality feedback. Peter, a school leader, who each year during the annual evaluation meeting with his direct reports, asks five questions.

Peter's Top 5 Questions to garner feedback:

1. Are you hopeful?
2. What do you like or appreciate the most about working here?
3. If you could change anything at our organization, what would it be?
4. What would give you pause about renewing your contract (or staying with the organization) another year?
5. What can I do to make it easier for you to work with me?

Their responses help him adapt his style and do more of what is working. Using this process might be a factor in why so many of his staffers stay on for years. With this practice along with his other feedback requests (e.g., about meeting quality or his decision-making), he has gotten better when offering corrective feedback that his people take to heart.

HOW TO GIVE FEEDBACK PEOPLE CAN USE

Like coaching, feedback is a conversation in which performance information is offered with the **goal of leading to a better path forward**. Before looking at a process for feedback, keep these things in mind about *quality feedback*. It is:

a. Regular and with a greater proportion positive than corrective (think 5/1 positive to corrective ratio at minimum).

b. Relevant, not trivial.

c. Thoughtful and planned so it is received as well as possible.

d. Grounded in "Why" it matters from the organizational perspective (not your personal one).

e. Almost always a two-way conversation between individuals who have established rapport. **It should feel like a dialogue between two adults**, not like a parent and child.

f. Not a prolonged emphasis on the past behavior (since the intent is to understand the past to find a better way forward).

g. Factual, not interpreted (avoids giving added meaning to the staffers' actual behavior or statements).

h. Specific (What, When, and the Impact).

i. Free of anxiety-producing language; maybe instead of saying "May I offer you some feedback?" use *advice, suggestions, or improvements.*

j. Descriptive, not judgmental, related to behaviors that the person can act on.

k. Humane—the better the relationship, the greater receptivity.

l. Delivered in a few ways, depending on the situation: quick on the spot, direct, or as a fuller coaching-style conversation.

m. Timely (with consideration for the right timing and place. The more complex, the greater the need for privacy).

n. Unbiased, nonjudgmental, and well intentioned.

Exercise: Check in. Using the letters above (a-n), which of the factors do you need to think about the most? ___ ___ __ ___ ____

Describe your experience with one of these factors.__________

____

____

____

Next, review how two feedback conversations broke down because the leader, as the feedback giver, used poor feedback practices.

Example #1: Leader interprets issue (see c, g, and n above)

Fact: Jamie walked in and out of the meeting numerous times, missing some information needed for his job.

Feedback with leader's assumptions and interpretation: *"I am disappointed that you left the meeting. The information was really important for you to hear. I guess you don't care about the work very much. It makes me wonder whether you are serious."* (Note how the leader climbs the Ladder of Inference, see page 53.)

Jamie: *"Wow. Here I was trying to be in the meeting as much as I could even though my daughter's school called to say she had an accident and had been rushed to the hospital."*

Confidence and trust between them eroded a bit since the leader did not *ask* why Jamie was leaving the meeting. The leader could have shown empathy and let Jamie decide how to get the information.

Example #2:

Fact: Alyssa fell short of her goal of raising enough sponsorship dollars to cover the costs of the special event.

Leader: *"Alyssa I'm not sure you have what it takes for this job. You missed the fundraising goal and caused everyone headaches. Maybe you don't have the drive or commitment. I'm going to give you one last chance; if you can't get it done, I will try someone else."*

Alyssa: *"I worked as hard as I could on this without much help. I asked for a previous donor list but never received it. I never said I had fundraising experience but wanted to help the organization by volunteering to do this. I thought I would get support. I worked 60 hours a week on this. I'm really stressed out."*

Result: Alyssa is deflated, and the leader has decreased confidence in her.... Unnecessarily, right?

Your thoughts:

What went well in example 2? ______________________________

____

How did the feedback approach likely make it harder to receive?

____

____

The leader might have said: "*Alyssa, you fell short of the fundraising goals. How do you feel about it? What do you think were the causes? What can you learn going forward? How can I better support you? What are your next steps to ensure greater success next time?*"

A feedback method. Next is a process to offer better feedback with suggested activities and thought processes that take place **before, during and after the feedback.**

The descriptions of *before, during and after* (on the next page) are useful whether the feedback is given during a planned meeting or on-the-spot. Until you get more natural providing it, consider the entire process, despite the time period you have. The level of detail depends on the feedback type, time, and setting. If the feedback is tough, consider the items carefully to ensure the best reception.

Before

- **Clarify the issue in your mind** (Is it worth addressing? If so, why? What is the specific issue? How does it impact the organization?
- **Set your mindset.** (Am I ready to be fully present, open, and to actively listen? Can I affirm it is not a personal peeve? Is it an issue I believe can be resolved? Am I able to treat this person as an adult and not like a child?)
- **Set intent for the interaction.** What is the result I hope for when offering the feedback?
- **Visualize success:** What does a successful feedback session look like? Mentally rehearse how you will help it be received well.
- **Choose a safe space:** Ensure you choose the right time and place.
- **Embrace a solution mindset**: I'm ready to spend most of our time on solutions, not dwelling on the errors (if it's corrective).

During

- **Establish rapport quickly.**
- **Begin the feedback** (either direct [see notes on next pages] or as a coaching conversation inquiring about their view of the situation). *"I'd like us to talk about the recent issue with xx or about xxxx."* (Be clear and specific.)

- **Ensure shared understanding of the issue** (what, when, where... factual and both of you are on the same page on the facts).
- **Share why it matters to the work** (i.e., the impact of their behavior; it's not about their personality).
- **Brainstorm solutions.** "*What ideas do you have on how to get to a better outcome when this type of situation arises in the future?*"
- **Agree on the actions to be taken and timelines.** "Let's agree on how you will move forward on this issue and set some timelines."
- **Decide what support is necessary to move forward** (from you and elsewhere).

- *Summarize and Close.*

After

- **Follow up periodically** on the actions.
- **Provide any needed support** and encouragement as they implement and carry out the feedback actions.
- **Offer thoughts on the impact of the changes**. Acknowledge when and what progress has taken place.

A feedback meeting example

Feedback Conversation

"I'd like to get your thoughts on how the project is going, and then, I'd like to share some suggestions and get your reactions to it."

Sample conversation questions:

Can you review the project goals?

What's worked well?

Where did you get stuck (if at all)?

What are you thinking about doing differently?

Here are a few thoughts on what I observed... (share what went well and what can be improved). Any reactions? (Listen to understand before responding).

So, what will you do to move forward on the project to help ensure its success?

In what ways do you need my support?

Thanks for your time and I look forward to seeing the needed progress on the project.

Whether affirming or corrective, feedback should lead to agreed up actions to continue or start doing. *What can you/we do to improve our chance of success in similar situations? How can you prepare to do this well in the future?*

On-the-spot quick feedback. On the spot feedback is just that—in the moment without much planning. Beware of using it when the situation is not conducive to high receptivity.

Here are some thoughts on the conditions for offering the best on-the-spot feedback:

1. when you have an existing trusting relationship,
2. it is useful feedback (but not earth shattering),
3. it is not new or shocking,
4. it is not a personal issue with you, and, or
5. it is not particularly challenging feedback nor hard for the person to receive and change.

Quick Feedback

Example 1:

Lanita, the way you handled the facilitation of the meeting was particularly good. Your organization, how you engaged everyone with good questions, and your wrap up with next steps were good. I look forward to more of that. Thanks.

Example 2:

Michael, when you arrived late again for the monthly meeting, I decided to give you this feedback before it sets in as a pattern. It disrupts the meeting, and you miss critical information. Please make sure you arrive on time for our monthly meetings. Do you need anything to make that happen?

When *direct* feedback is better than a conversation.

As we get better at providing feedback, we learn to distinguish "how" we provide it, using a feedback conversation or by being directive. Some cases where direct feedback ("just say it") would be fine.

- Time is limited, a good rapport exists, and it is important.
- Conversations in which the staffer tends to be evasive, rationalizes behavior constantly, or has low self-awareness. If the feedback is critical, you may need to provide it directly.

- When performance expectations are non-negotiable. Tell them directly, then prompt them to share what support they will need to carry out the tasks.

Exercise: Two real work feedback applications

A. Think of a real work situation where providing positive feedback is warranted.

1. Who needs the feedback?	
2. What is the specific affirming feedback?	
3. Why does it matter for the work or the organization?	
4. When and where will you offer it?	
1. What is the mutually beneficial outcome you want from the feedback?	
5. Other considerations?	

B. Now think about a real work situation where corrective feedback is warranted.

2. Who needs the feedback?	
3. What is the specific corrective feedback about?	
4. What is the impact on your unit's goals?	

5. When and where will you provide this feedback?	
6. How will you keep it a two-way, productive conversation?	
7. What is the mutually beneficial outcome you want from the feedback?	

Deliver the feedback then reflect here: After planning and delivering the above feedback, complete this worksheet[31]:

	What worked?	**What to improve next time**
Process		
Planning the feedback		
Engaging in the feedback		
Sharing thoughts about the key issues		
Listening		
Creating action plan		
Relationship		
Communication quality		
Staffers' reaction		
Level of mutual respect		

[31] Adapted from p. 52, Harvard Business Review Press, Giving Effective Feedback, 20 Minute Manager, 2014

Results		
Progress on changes/actions		
Impact of the change		

Keep practicing. We all can get better in this area.

This closes the COACH Key, chapters 6 and 7. Before moving to the DEVELOP Key, take time to affirm your readiness to use coaching-style leadership to enable your team to deliver their best work.

Make Coaching a Reflexive Practice, becoming unconsciously competent (i.e., you do not have to think about it; it's natural).

Exercise: Five affirming habits. Place a check in the circles of the ones where you can say a definite YES.

- ❍ I recognize the benefits of shifting from constant bossing (telling) to two-way coaching conversations to foster growth.
- ❍ I am confident behavior change can happen, and I know it requires more than one conversation. So, I will acknowledge incremental growth.
- ❍ I aim for all my feedback to be about behavior, not the person, and tied to the impact on the work and organization.
- ❍ I build positive rapport with my team members in an ongoing way, allowing for better receptivity to coaching and feedback.
- ❍ I commit to offer ongoing feedback, with much more positive than corrective. I am unafraid of offering both.

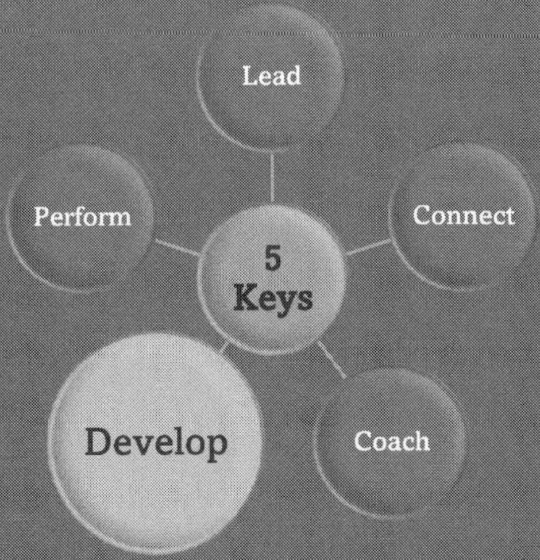

the DEVELOP key

The "People Smart" Leader consistently develops the talents of their staffers through varied activities to ready them for greater innovation, advancement, and motivation.

The Develop Key: Growing Your People Pays Off

"I'm outdone at how little they know about things that I think are pretty basic."

A new leader repeatedly used these words as she lamented about the team she inherited. I asked if these were skills that they were capable of learning. "Well, of course," she replied. "Then teach them or have someone else do it."

Expecting team members to magically "know" what to do, what you expect, or how to do an entirely new task doesn't seem logical. But it happens. And, believing they want to continue what they've always done without stretching and advancing is also faulty.

Activating the Develop Key begins with acknowledging development is an essential and rewarding aspect of leading people to do their best work. Development means ongoing learning. It is the *deliberate habit of sharpening your people's (and your) technical skills and enhancing professional behaviors to maintain and increase value.*

Futurist Alvin Toffler spoke in the 70s of this challenge of 21st Century leaders, if they fail to let go of old modes of thinking to learn and embrace better ones.

"The illiterate of the 21st Century will not be those who cannot read and write, but those who cannot learn, unlearn and relearn."

The Develop Key includes two chapters. **Chapter 8** helps you move your people to the next level of competence. Then **Chapter 9** centers on team dynamics, development, and synergies for performance.

Chapter 8

Develop Each, Develop All

This chapter covers Develop topics that will contribute to better work results and fulfillment.

1. Develop each and all of your team using a range of options.
2. Delegation can be a great way to develop people.
3. Make your meetings purposeful and skill enhancing.

A story to make the case:

"For more than two years, I've been so busy multi-tasking and putting out fires that I haven't done much to stay on top of the current trends in my field. I must prioritize joining a peer network, reading, going to at least one key conference, and figure out what AI has to do with our work. I can feel I'm falling behind. If I don't do something, I may wake up one day and be told I'm no longer useful."

This marketing executive had kept her head buried in the tedium of the never-ending tasks that demanded her time. She began to feel less competent in her specialty area. Her awakening: She needed to develop her skills for the changing work environment. Good for her.

Re-invigorating your staff, innovating, and planning for the future of your work are within your reach when you commit to ongoing self and staff development. **To develop your people means creating**

conditions for them to grow, learn, enhance their skills and attributes purposefully.

You should assume your team members want to increase their skills, feel like they are meaningfully contributing, and have pathways to advance in their roles. Take a moment to think about the case for developing your people as part of your leadership strategy.

The case for and benefits of ongoing development:

- Meet new requirements when organizational goals change. That typically involves some level of staff reskilling and upskilling, to deliver on those goals.
- Keep pace with the changing demands of your stakeholders.
- Prepare people for long-term success and value, avoiding skill stagnation in a dynamic work environment, *futureproofing*.
- Demonstrate to your direct reports that you believe in their current and *future* capacity to contribute more.
- Increase attraction and retention of talented staff—ward off boredom or stagnation- factors in active and "quiet quitting."
- Improve work productivity—better skilled, more motivated, better work results.
- Prepare your team members to advance along their desired career pathways.

DEVELOP EACH AND ALL WITH A RANGE OF OPTIONS

To maximize your team's performance, devote time to individual, team, and your own development. Periodically ask yourself: *Am I helping to maximize the potential of each person and the collective team? Am I developing new leaders to take the organization into the future? Am I creating more meaning for the staffers?*

Exercise: My current support of staff development

Place your direct reports initials in the first column. In the second column, make brief notes about what you and they have done (or not) over the last 12 months. For the third column, indicate the purpose of these development activities, such as readiness for promotion, to (or improve upon) a needed new skill, build people aptitudes, explore innovation. In the fourth column, indicate if these activities proved valuable to the staffer and the work by writing Y or N.

Name	Development activities this year	Purpose	Value Y/N

When you look at your responses, what message do they send about your focus on staff development?

Lack of development is one factor in employee turnover. And the cost of staff replacement is high—at least 30% of a staff person's annual salary (consider: vacation payouts, severance, relocation, signing bonuses, lost productivity during role vacancy, etc.)

On the other hand, read the positive feedback from staffers following a professional development session, one in a series of ongoing developmental initiatives.

"The whole endeavor was so powerful. The fact that the organization finds it important for us to work on ourselves individually first for the good of the whole team is refreshing and wise! I liken it to how houses need foundations to be laid first in order for them to stand—same principle for us. I'm grateful to be a part of the organization."

Low-cost, high value results of development. There are many methods to ensure your staffers keep pace with any new job skill requirements or sustain their work vitality and creativity. All staff, whether new, tenured, moderate performers, or high performers, should be a part of your staff development plans.

Gather input on development needs and wants. To be most effective, devise staff development plans as a joint effort between you and your staff members. Design the plan with the organization, team, and each staff person in mind.

- Meet with each person to learn of their growth and learning passion and needs related to their job role and career interest. Then create the plan, invest the resources, and execute.
- Meet with your entire team to brainstorm a list of learning themes and activities that would be helpful to better deliver the team's goals and increase everyone's overall skills.
- Include professional development objectives when doing annual goal setting.
- Set aside time to debrief learning activities to prompt staffers to apply new learning to their work or make space for the staffer to share insights with other team members.

Many ways to develop your people, so cost is not a barrier. Think of development as divided into two major categories: 1) **enhancing employees' professional behaviors** and 2) **increasing their technical skills.** In addition, development opportunities should be provided to each person, and others should be for the whole team to ensure a baseline of knowledge that affects everyone's work, relationships, norms, and mindsets.

This following sampling of development options includes some that have no financial cost, so there is no reason not to continually invest in your people. Look it over.

20 Options	Brief Description	Cost
1. Delegate higher-level task	Coach and empower on task for next level skills	None
2. Virtual conferences	Online events	No or low
3. Assessments (leadership, style, etc.)	Build awareness, clarify skill needs for growth	low
4. Mentor or shadow (peer or more senior)	Assign a good match with someone skilled/experienced in areas of interest	No or low
5. Job rotation or sharing	Broaden skillset and collaboration by rotating tasks	Low
6. Coaching	Provide individual coaching to enhance professional behaviors	Moderate, budgeted
7. Professional networks	Either internal or external, related to skill area	No, low
8. Stretch assignments	Assignments beyond the job requirements, to learn and take risks, innovate	No or low
9. Employee resource groups	Internal, local, or regional memberships	No or low
10. Learning circles or book clubs (topical)	Within or outside team; shared topics, readings, blogs, etc., make meaning, choose frequency	No
11. Committees or special task forces	Special, limited term issues-study a process or tool development	No
12. Career planning and progression support	Career mapping and developmental opportunities, championing for new roles	No
13. Multiday conferences	Off-site or virtual conferences, expand skills and network	Moderate, budgeted
14. Formal education	Degree completion over some years	Higher, budgeted
15. Free conferences during the workday	Half or full-day conferences hosted by reputable organizations	No
16. Networking event invites	Out of work time themed events to meet key people, build network	No or low
17. Online course subscriptions	Skill building subscription services to build competencies	Low
18. Certifications	Short-term training events to earn job or career credentials	Moderate, budgeted
19. Lunch and learns	One hour lunch, high impact topical presenters (onsite or off)	No or low
20. Site visits to peer organizations	One or multi-day visits or shadowing at organizations with similar roles to learn, innovate	Low to Moderate

Exercise: Making application

1. Which of the items (or others) on page 191 might you select for individual team members over the next six months?

Direct Report	Option #(s) above or theirs, and detail
Ex. S. Jones	#7, 8, 20: *Join HR network, develop new employee engagement survey, plan, and visit Sr. HR director at a local business with strong engagement scores*

2. Which can you integrate into collective team learning to build competencies and improve team relationships for everyone?

   a. ______________________________

   b. ______________________________

   c. ______________________________

DELEGATION CAN BE GREAT FOR DEVELOPMENT

An unwillingness or inability to let go of some of your *favorite* tasks or projects and successfully delegate them to the next level staff can stunt you and your team members' growth. It's easy, and a trap, to do what you've always done—jump in there and manage the activities you used to do, especially those you loved.

Story: Reluctance to let go and delegate

An assistant principal, who used to be a classroom teacher, was known to add extra touches for students in an effort to create a positive classroom environment. Putting up student artwork, planning field trips and competitions, shopping for trophies and costume parties, and such energized her. Now, in her higher, more strategic role, she continues these same tasks while stressing about not having enough time to do her real work. As our coaching progressed, her focus became elevating her work by spending more time on the strategic level of school performance, and letting go to delegate tasks to others and ensuring they were done effectively. The two teachers to whom the tasks were eventually delegated experienced a burst of new energy because the assignments offered variety and boosted their project planning skills.

Poor or no delegation is a common issue with new leaders. It's a sign that you are not discerning the work you should be giving your attention to and what your staff members can and should do.

Poor delegators are usually plagued by one or a combination of these:

- Still tied to and comfortable doing the transactional and tactical work they performed before moving to a higher level.

- Have little experience or skill delegating appropriately to prepare their people to perform new tasks as expected.

- They don't trust, don't know, or feel threatened by their staff's abilities. "Giving it to them will make me look incompetent."

- They get a lot of satisfaction from tasks that were a part of an earlier role. In such cases, the elevated leader can seek other ways to fulfill themselves.

Delegation can be highly rewarding, signaling that you believe in and value your direct reports' contributions. As the leader, it allows you to elevate your leadership game. So, delegation is a powerful development strategy for the leader and their staffers.

Get started with better delegation.

- Think about *why* you feel compelled to "do it all." What are you avoiding by not delegating? ______________________

  ____

- Start small initially. Identity one task that you really need to delegate because others can do it, and it is likely the farthest below the tasks you are paid to perform.

- Jot down the "satisfactory" results you want from this task you will be letting go. (Be careful not to include things that are specific to how you do it; focus on the needed results.)

- Jot down what tasks or action steps will be required for the person to whom it will be delegated to do the task well.

- Try this process outlined below to help make it effective.

Exercise: Delegation Process and Practice

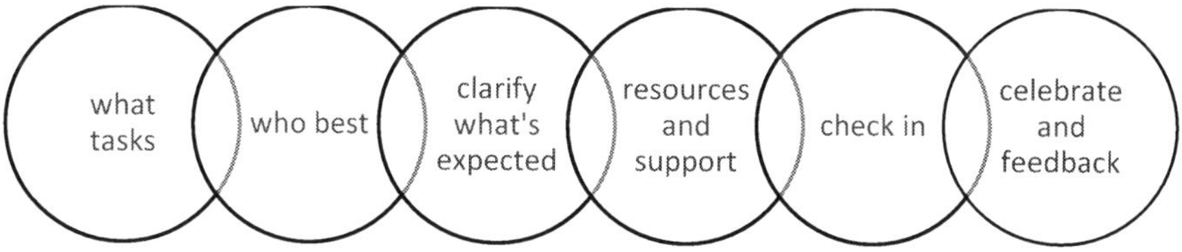

Apply this process to a task that you will delegate soon.

What to delegate and to whom

1. What needs to and should be delegated related to you and your team's work?	
2. What steps or actions are involved in completing this task?	
3. Who is the best person to do it?	

Assign and clarify resources.

4. How and when will you assign the task?	
5. What are the expectations, timeline, and boundaries you will communicate?	
6. What is their level of autonomy (be sure to share that with them)?	
7. What resources will you provide?	

Monitor, support, and celebrate.

8. How should you check in through the process to address progress, support and fix any challenges?	
9. What will you do to acknowledge success and continue the staffers' growth?	

A testimony from a newer mid-level leader*:*
"Using this delegation activity on a real work task that I needed to delegate helped me think through how to do it, and it went well, and now I can pay attention to some things I've neglected."

The benefits are greater than the costs. While delegation doesn't necessarily have much cost from a financial perspective, it does require you to allocate a bit of time initially to ensure you delegate well, in a way that both inspires the team member being tasked and provides what they need to do the task successfully.

Focus on the advantages of good, developmental delegation:

- Allows staff to build new or engage more of existing skills.
- May lead to more innovative ways to do tasks.
- Puts leader in the role of a people developer rather than a *hands-in-everything* manager.
- Frees leader to do tasks more compatible with their role.

- Demonstrates leader's emotional maturity to let go of passion projects and their precise way of doing them.

BETTER MEETINGS—PURPOSEFUL AND DEVELOPMENTAL

Meetings are costly and time-consuming. They can offer everyone more by being well structured and a vehicle to foster ongoing learning to keep pace and ahead of changing workplace needs. Meetings can be used to keep staff members abreast of current trends, better practices, new modes of thinking and delivering services.

One leader of a large non-profit was experiencing a high degree of interpersonal conflicts on the executive team. There were disparate viewpoints that appeared to have no chance of reaching consensus. Individuals were stuck in their views. Camps developed quickly, with one subgroup sparring with the other. I asked: "How do you and your team learn? What are you learning together?" The client responded, "Our people are always busy doing their own work." Over time, after some convincing, they began integrating small bursts of team learning and development into the typically overlong meetings to which they were accustomed. As they began debriefing short articles, learning communication styles, researching and sharing industry trends, sharing a podcast on collaboration processes, their meetings became more productive and shorter!

The range of adverse effects of a non-learning environment:

- ✓ People become confidently entrenched in their faulty views due to lack of exposure to better and "informed" perspectives.

- ✓ The leader must spend extra time addressing issues individually since the team hasn't learned to generate solutions collaboratively with their peers.

- ✓ There is not a set of baseline skills and knowledge across the team to inform actions, norms, and decisions. So, the culture can gradually deteriorate.

Create powerful, productive, growth-producing meetings by using a few easy-to-implement changes.

- First, recognize bad meetings aren't free! There are the costs of staff being away from their actual work, the cost of low morale from time-wasting meetings, the cost of lack of clarity due to meetings that are not purposeful, and more.

- Be sure you have a reason to meet. If not, relieve everyone of attending a meeting that is likely going nowhere.

- Perform a "meeting audit" in which you list all of your recurring meetings, clarify their purpose, frequency, time frame, participants, platform, and roles. Determine how to maximize the value of each. Eliminate, shorten or change the frequency of those that aren't delivering the best return on the investment of time and resources they absorb. Make changes needed to break the "meeting to meeting" common routine.

- Include the right people in meetings; don't waste time requiring people who either don't know the subject matter or whose jobs aren't related to it. Give them a break.

- Pay attention to the best reasons to meet:
    - Decision-making that produces concrete choices.
    - Learning/educational events.
    - Working meetings to share ideas and produce something. The outputs might be generation of ideas, consensus around impending decisions or changes, or better coordination. Ask people to spend a bit of time preparing before the meeting to bring more depth and thought.
    - Team strengthening, to develop interpersonal and organizational skills, creating cross-team alignment.
- **Meetings that only share information rarely require in-person presence.** Virtual tools and email work well.
- For every meeting, the convener should clarify its purpose to everyone (both in advance and at the start of the meeting)—why everyone is here and what 's to be accomplished by the end. This helps people prepare to participate meaningfully.
- Make the meeting efficient (i.e., with the most accomplished with the least wasted efforts and resources) to free up more time for learning. For each meeting, think about: *Is this worth a 60-minute investment of our time or is 30 minutes enough? How can we maximize the time assigned to each topic? How can we structure daylong gatherings to ensure we accomplish something defined and meaningful, engage everyone, leave people inspired and with follow up actions?*

With improved, more purposeful meetings, you can **embed learning and development** in them. Consider these for a start:

- Select books or other materials to learn about industry trends, peer organization strategies, leadership skills, problem solving, decision making, leading others, etc. Allow staff members to help choose these strong topics.
- Allocate 15-30 minutes of meeting time periodically to delve into ideas from the reading, video, or podcast. Either engage the whole team or break into pairs, then report back. Basic questions to guide the conversation (or create your own):
  - *What were the author's biggest ideas?*
  - *Which ideas related directly to our work?*
  - *What actions can we take to enhance our work?*
- Seek feedback. Periodically, ask the team for ways to enhance learning and make the overall meetings more meaningful.

Reflect and Plan: What one or two ways can I make our meetings better, more productive, and developmental (growth oriented)?

This closes the first of two chapters related to The DEVELOP key. Chapter 9 addresses developing your direct reports into a synergistic, high performing team.

Develop and Sustain Team Capabilities

Team development strategies, essential for quality results:

1. Developing the team is multi-faceted, ongoing, essential.
2. Conduct team assessment and norm-setting.
3. Reset the team culture for new goals or new people.
4. Sample team development activities.

The People Smart leader knows their team's interpersonal dynamics along with their collective skill set will either enhance or diminish performance. Leaders ask themselves: Do my staffers' productivity and dispositions, when combined, lead us to our required results? Does the state of the team inspire everyone to do their best work?

"Even though individual members may be well-prepared and capable in their individual roles, there is often a sizable deficit when it comes to the overall leadership team's collective capability."[32]

TEAM DEVELOPMENT: MULTI-FACETED, ONGOING, ESSENTIAL

Look at three common misconceptions about what it takes to install and maintain quality teams. Do you hold either of these views?

[32] Cahill. A. March 2020. Ccl.org. Are you getting the best out of your senior leadership team?

1) The belief that a collection of high achieving individuals *automatically* turns into a high performing team.

2) Thinking that holding a once annual team building session, then repeat it in with some variation a year later, is enough.

3) A belief that employees will figure out how to work together productively without purposeful development.

There are **two major areas for ongoing team development:**

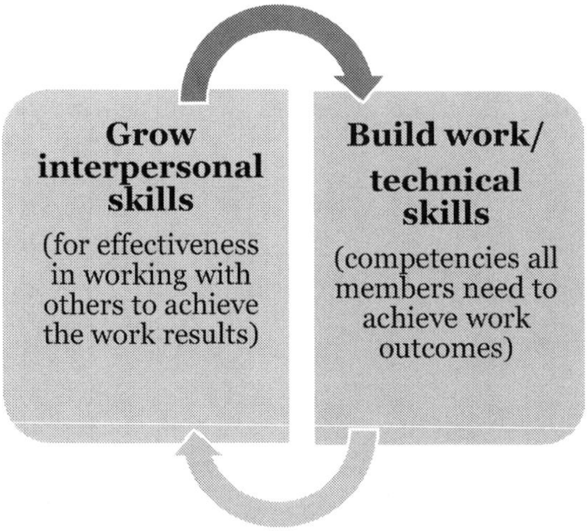
Grow interpersonal skills
(for effectiveness in working with others to achieve the work results)
Build work/ technical skills
(competencies all members need to achieve work outcomes)

What seems most damaging to work groups is deficient people skills. Sometimes the highest performing individuals are the least effective working with the team. Other times, people are so unwilling to collaborate and share information that they end up working at cross-purposes or duplicating work, to the organization's detriment.

I recently read that *only one in five teams is high performing*. So, if your team needs work, you have company, and ought to approach development as mining untapped potential. It also means that your team might welcome attention to how they function together.

During the launch of a professional development series, with a team that had been demoralized by the previous leader, I and the new leader assumed the participants would be tentative about self-disclosing in what they called a low-trust environment. Yet, as the conversations focused on "Who's on the team? What is their contribution? And how does their role intersect with mine?" the air became lighter, and their engagement was high and energetic. At day's end (with the energy still high), participants remarked that they shared more of themselves than they expected and felt good about it. They asked for more chances to become more aware of other team members and themselves, their strengths and skill gaps.

Recognize signs of low functioning teams, which affect both achieving results and staff morale. Do any apply to your team?

- ☑ Missed deadlines.
- ☑ Working at cross purposes.
- ☑ Projects stalled.
- ☑ Team members disengaged.
- ☑ Topics addressed over and over without resolve.
- ☑ Staff turnover.
- ☑ Tolerance of low performance.
- ☑ Conflict avoidance.
- ☑ Subgroup loyalties.
- ☑ High defensiveness.
- ☑ Unequal workloads and expectations.
- ☑ Unable to reach consensus.
- ☑ Reluctance to seek help from each other.
- ☑ Blaming each other.
- ☑ Lots of sidebar conversations and gossip.
- ☑ Complaints of unfairness.
- ☑ Groupthink valued over diverse thinking.
- ☑ Busy work prioritized over results.
- ☑ Competing for favor or authority.
- ☑ Erosion in professional behavior.
- ☑ Projects lack direction and focus.

- ☑ Patterns of unresolved conflicts.
- ☑ Duplicated work; redundant processes.
- ☑ Silence in meetings, meeting dread.
- ☑ Personality clashes.
- ☑ Absenteeism.
- ☑ Key information not shared.
- ☑ Low transparency in meetings.

Use this space to record any of these signs that are showing up right now on your team that could interfere with performance and staff motivation. (A combination of two or more of these factors signals you likely need to give your team functioning some attention.)

____

____

____

Prioritize time for team development: There are many touchpoints a leader has with their team members. So, as a start, think about how to use these existing interactions to grow healthier team habits. Then as you see the returns on these investments, do more.

Here are some places to build team development into your normal work life:

- ☑ During regular meetings, set aside 10-15 minutes for team bonding. There are easy-to-find activities for this on the Internet, and you can rotate leading this among the team.
- ☑ Set up in-person or virtual paired "coffee chats," rotating year-round, allowing teammates to get to know each other.

☑ Engage in quick problem solving in which a team member presents the group with a challenge they are facing, and the team spends 10-15 minutes brainstorming solutions. The member then shares their thoughts about the suggestions.

☑ Brainstorm ideas on how to make the team or the work processes better, (10-15 minutes during a meeting).

☑ Have everyone take a behavior style assessment and share with each other to show the strengths existing in the team. Then, find ways to better engage these strengths in the work.

☑ Quick celebrations: Occasionally use 10 minutes or so of meeting time for work bright spots, celebrations, milestones in life, vacation highlights, etc.

☑ Set up voluntary out of office social times or service projects.

☑ Plan annual or semi-annual off-sites (retreats), with a specific theme or objective. Allow your team to co-create the plans.

☑ Do quick checks at the start of meeting: such as, *What part of your work are you looking forward to this week? What was the most fulfilling part of last week's work? What has you scratching your head right now about your work?*

TEAM ASSESSMENT AND NORM-SETTING

The graphic that follows, and the accompanying descriptions identify suggested tasks to foster collaborative, positive work relationships while achieving high quality outputs and outcomes.

Key Team Development Tasks

(based on themes from various team development models)

Brief descriptions:

1. **Vision:** Be sure the organization's or department's vision and social purpose do not fade into the background. This is the team's anchor that continually invigorates everyone around this larger unifying direction. The leader consistently frames their efforts around this grand purpose.

2. **Shared Goals and Outcomes**: Closely related to and in support of vision is ensuring each person knows the team's collective goals and everyone's specific role, value, and results that tie to the goals. Figure out ways to keep the goals alive among the team year-round.

3. **Composition and Role Alignment**: This is about "who is on the team"—their skills, responsibilities, intersections with others' roles, special talents, and preferences. Clarify how each person's role interacts with the others to reduce duplication and coordinate the goal-related work. Encourage the team to strengthen collaborative capacities and integrate team members' talents to move projects forward.

4. **Team State—Current to Future:** Activities should be planned to assess: "Where are we now? Where do we need to go?" There are tools easily accessible to assess the team's state, including some in the next section of this chapter.

5. **Team Learning**: Since all team members need to build professional/emotional and technical skills, consider: *What new technical skills do we need in order to deliver excellence in our changing work environment? How do we collectively mature our behaviors and communication? What learning activities or tools will grow our E.I., build cohesion, resolve conflicts, and more?* Using validated instruments can be useful when facilitated well to foster appreciation for everyone's styles and talents.

6. **Norming and Onboarding (New Members)**: Here you set up operating agreements (norms) and a team charter (see Activity #4 at end of this chapter for a sample). Norms address agreements on all or more of these: how the team behaves with each other, holds everyone accountable, makes decisions, engages in meetings, resolves conflict, and defines quality results to create the team's high-performance culture. When new members join the team, provisions are made to integrate them into the team culture and norms.

7. **Assess and Revitalize**: Team members collectively evaluate the team's outcomes, processes, and health, then decide how to revitalize the team when the context changes or they stray from its charter agreements.

Assess the team's current and future state.

There are a variety of ways to assess how well your team is functioning and set goals for your team development efforts. Activity #1 at the end of this chapter is an example. The leader can also use the "Team Observation Checklist," (Activity #2 at the end of the chapter) to make notes about what you observe during and after a team meeting or other gatherings. Using this tool can be helpful since we often get accustomed to how things are and rarely stop and reflect on meeting processes, what voices are heard, which are not, how decisions are made (or whether they are made at all.). Then Activity #3 can be used for individual team members to assess, reflect, and choose a behavior change to hone their teaming capacities.

Research from Teams Unleashed[33] describes four discrete types of teams using two broad areas: productivity and positivity.

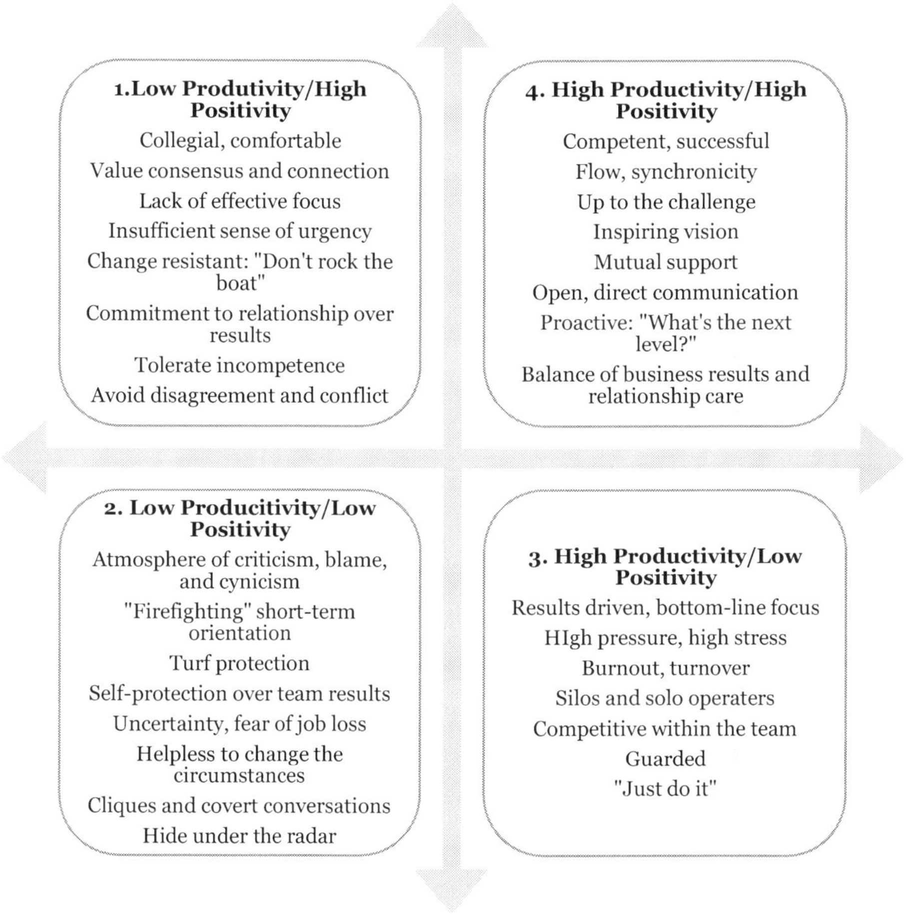
1.Low Produtivity/High Positivity
Collegial, comfortable
Value consensus and connection
Lack of effective focus
Insufficient sense of urgency
Change resistant: "Don't rock the boat"
Commitment to relationship over results
Tolerate incompetence
Avoid disagreement and conflict
4. High Productivity/High Positivity
Competent, successful
Flow, synchronicity
Up to the challenge
Inspiring vision
Mutual support
Open, direct communication
Proactive: "What's the next level?"
Balance of business results and relationship care
2. Low Producitivity/Low Positivity
Atmosphere of criticism, blame, and cynicism
"Firefighting" short-term orientation
Turf protection
Self-protection over team results
Uncertainty, fear of job loss
Helpless to change the circumstances
Cliques and covert conversations
Hide under the radar
3. High Productivity/Low Positivity
Results driven, bottom-line focus
HIgh pressure, high stress
Burnout, turnover
Silos and solo operaters
Competitive within the team
Guarded
"Just do it"

After reviewing all four quadrants closely, which of the four best reflects your team's current state and what makes you say that?

---

[33] Sandahl, P. and Phillips, A. 2019.

Achieving equilibrium, when both productivity and positivity are present and balanced, is among a leader's top development aims.

What's the team's future state? Your next step, after assessing the current state of the team, is to determine the factors your team development should target and make plans to move towards that better, future state.

Exercise: Pause here and make notes on the areas you and the team will target to arrive at your future state. The selected 3-4 areas that, when improved, will have the greatest positive influence on the team's productivity and interpersonal relationships are:

1.
2.
3.
4.

Team norms and charter

It is important to get all team members to coalesce around key elements to shape a healthy team culture. A team charter is valuable in that regard. *It is a simple roadmap that captures the team's agreements about their mutual purpose, goals, and how to best work together.* Developing the charter brings together the thinking and strengths of all team members. The chartering process allows the team to move any whispered complaints and unexpressed ideas for improvement into meaningful conversations and actions about the team's operating environment. Once complete, the charter becomes a powerful tool for getting everyone *to move in the same direction,* and it serves as a yardstick to hold everyone accountable without losing their individual uniqueness.

About Team Norms and Charters:

- ☑ Develop the charter early in the relationship of the leader and their direct reports. Without clarity, free-developing team patterns will emerge, including some that are hard to correct.

- ☑ Plan one or more facilitated team sessions to draft the team charter. Use a set of questions, which the team decides are the most critical to answer. (See the sample questions in Activity #4 and modify to meet your team's context.)

- ☑ Keep the charter alive and visible. How will you do that? Will you keep it posted in your meeting room, include it on agendas, or hand it out occasionally for reinforcement?

- ☑ Review the norms and charter at least annually to determine the extent to which the team is meeting its own expectations. Decide if the operating norms need adjusting. Revise or replace the norms if they are no longer useful.

RESET THE TEAM CULTURE FOR NEW GOALS OR PEOPLE

Bruce Tuckman's[34] 1965 classic stages of team development is a good mental model for assessing how your team is situated at any given

---

[34] Developmental sequence in small groups. Psychological Bulletin. 63(6) 384-399.

time. Astute leaders know that they will need to revisit the stages as internal and external events affect the health and performance of the team. Even a well-established workgroup can face changes that signal a need to recalibrate aspects related to earlier stages, which means *re*-forming, *re*-storming and or *re*-norming.

Tuckman's Team Stages in Brief:

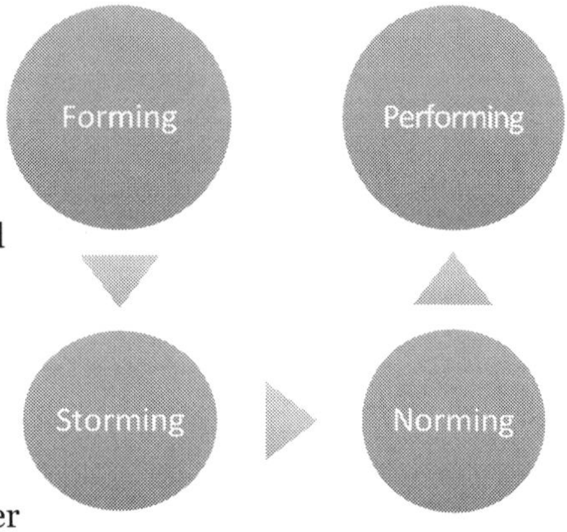

1. **Forming**. Individuals are just coming together and trying to get to know each other. They begin learning each other's stories and styles, roles, schedules, etc.

2. **Storming**. The is often the most challenging of the stages, wherein members have gotten to know each other, and inevitably styles clash with the leader and each other emerge. The leader helps the team members manage the frictions and re-focuses everyone on the goals. Avoidance of "storming" needs (e.g., trust building, conflict and collaboration skill development) can trap the team in this stage and set up a culture of dysfunction.

3. **Norming**. After team members have explored and learned to negotiate their conflicts, the team begins to crystallize, and a healthier culture begins taking root. Team members appreciate their differences and work together. The leader facilitates norming by chartering the team, encouraging engagement, aiming everyone towards shared goals, celebrating successes, and creating a sense of community.

4. **Performing**. Here, the team is fully functional, and members can manage their relationships, work toward shared goals, communicate openly, experience a sense of belonging, and achieve quality results. All of this can happen without the leader's constant intervention.

Check in: In which of the stages do you believe your team is currently situated or are you seeing a blend of two? __________

____

The most common causes of destabilization of the team culture, thus requiring reassessment, are 1) when *new goals* are established, 2) *team composition* changes (people join or exit the team) and 3) when team agreements have been transgressed without accountability.

Resetting for entering and exiting staff: When the team composition changes, some disruption usually occurs. Team members often "feel" the difference (even if unexpressed), and that "feel" can vary depending on *who* enters or exits and their impact on the atmosphere. Re-setting the culture need not be painful once you recognize the team needs to do a bit of re-forming and re-norming.

Think about this story: *A senior leader's presence on the executive team was clearly a positive ingredient in four key areas of the team culture: 1) attending to inclusiveness of diverse perspectives as they wrestled with tough issues, 2) setting steps and assignments at the end of all meetings, 3) encouraging fuller participation rather than going with the most dominant member's views during decision-making, and 4) spending time recognizing the individual and team accomplishments and bright spots in the work.*

When this leader left the organization for a higher-level job, the team at first didn't realize why there began to be so much conflict and undercurrents among members, why the meetings seemed to not resolve anything, and why they began dreading the senior staff meetings. They later recognized the exit of a member shifted the team dynamics and effectiveness. Becoming aware of this, then working to figure out what is missing in the team, provided a pathway to reset the culture for better results.

Resetting for new goals: If the organization's goals or strategies require shifts in their way of working, the team needs to reconsider the needed changes together. For example, if the organization finds itself facing financial losses, or chooses new program strategies, it may be necessary to ask: *What do these changes require in how we work together? What do we need to stop or start doing? How do the changes impact our pace, structures, processes, priorities, and engagement?* In such a situation, you will want to refine the shared goals, outcomes, norms, and charter to align with the new objectives and re-position the team for performance excellence.

This closes Chapter 9 of The Develop Key, which helps you put in place a high performing, synergized, and highly satisfied team.

Before leaving the two DEVELOP KEY chapters, review the sample tools for developing your team. You may find one or two of the six on the following pages helpful.

Be reminded that developing your staffers, individually and as a team, goes a long way to achieving exceptional work results and keeping people engaged, growing, and inspired.

SIX SAMPLE TEAM TOOLS

Activity 1: Assessing the current team state.

What is already present in your team's culture? Use the 18 characteristics below as a checklist (You can also ask team members to assess the team using checklist or rating each on scale of 1-5. Compile the results, share themes, honor what is working, and choose a few areas for development).

Work Productivity Attributes

1. ☐ **A clear and shared vision and values** is regularly articulated, the shared "Why" which connects the team emotionally to their roles, goals, and the organization.

2. ☐ **Achieving shared results** through measurable, timebound deadlines and aligned tasks across the team

3. ☐ **Effective team leadership** in which the leader uses their role to keep the vision in the forefront, remove barriers, support team growth, and share leadership to build team member competencies and put the best expertise up front.

4. ☐ **Supportive structures and processes** are in place for team members to do their work.

5. ☐ **Roles and responsibilities are clear**, including how they interact and enable all to achieve shared goals.

6. ☐ A **Culture of accountability** is understood and embraced by all in pursuit of achieving shared goals.

7. ☐ **Diverse team composition with aligned functions** reflects complementary and varied styles and expertise to achieve goals. The team size should be manageable to provide time and resources to all.

8. ☐ A **defined way of working and making decisions**. Created by the team, the charter clarifies how team values are expressed in our behavioral norms and team processes.

9. ☐ **Culture of learning** allows team to increase expertise and excellence, never resting on current knowledge.

Positive Culture Attributes

10. ☐ A keen sense of **interdependence and trust** exists--enabling sharing practices, thinking and feelings.

11. ☐ **Inclusivity** is valued, where a range of styles, ideas, perspectives, and skills are seen as enablers of team thriving.

12. ☐ There is a sense of **emotional safety** wherein team members share feelings, thoughts, and vulnerabilities.

13. ☐ Members experience **social connection** including friendship, fun and belonging.

14. ☐ **Effective communication** keeps everyone abreast of plans and progress, and there are formal and informal means for storytelling and sharing the right information.

15. ☐ **Stretching beyond the ordinary**—members take on new risks, stretch to grow, and increase thriving during adversity.

16. ☐ **Appreciation and optimism** are evident in celebrating successes and recognizing team members along the way.

17. ☐ There is **high quality interaction** in which members make sure everyone is involved, each voice is honored and never drowned out by other members.

18. ☐ **Planning and preparation** are the norms, with effective, inclusive mechanisms, processes, input, and feedback.

Checkpoint: Which 3 to 4 of these should be your first priorities?

____

____

Activity 2: Team Dynamics Observation Checklist

You can do this exercise or assign a team member to confidentially take an observer role during a meeting or retreat. Use a simple rating, such as 1-5, with one the lowest and 5 the highest. Follow-up by sharing observations with the team and choosing actionable ways to enhance a few critical areas.

Area	Notes	Rating
COMMUNICATION		
1. Who talks? How long? How often?		
2. Who do people look at when they speak?		
3. Who talks with whom? Who interrupts whom?		
4. What style of communication is used? (assertions, questions, tone, gestures, etc.)		
5. How well is conflict managed?		
PARTICIPATION		
6. Who are the high participants?		
7. Low participants?		
8. Any noticeable shifts in participation?		
9. Who keeps things going? Why?		
10. How is the group in terms of bullying and shutting down others' ideas?		
11. How are silent people treated? How is silence interpreted?		
DECISION-MAKING		
12. Do conversations lead to decisions/actions or is the group inclined towards indecision?		
13. Does the group drift from topic to topic? Who topic jumps?		
14. Is there effort to get all members participating in decisions?		

15. Are decisions pushed through by a majority or an individual despite objections?		
16. Are there people who make contributions that do not receive a response or recognition?		
17. Who supports other members' decisions or suggestions? How does this affect others?		
ROLES: WHO PLAYS WHICH?		
18. Task, focused on getting things done		
19. Maintenance: focused on improving relationships among members		
20. Self-oriented: focused on personal needs despite group concerns		
LEADERSHIP		
21. How does leader engage to help group be more effective?		
22. Is there excessive deference to the leader?		
23. Who are the informal leaders?		
24. Which leader competencies play well in the team?		
25. Which leader attributes need to improve when with the team?		

Overall observations:

Recommendations:

Activity 3: Individual Team Skills Self-Assessment

Ought people get excited about being on a team with me?

My team skills.... Circle the attributes below that you are confident you have and demonstrate.

1. Adaptable
2. Open to different perspectives
3. Prepared
4. Participatory
5. Supportive of team members
6. Reliable to complete my share of tasks
7. Team goals guide my perspective during conversations
8. Awareness of my strengths and limitations
9. Good emotional management
10. Courageous and constructive in raising issues
11. Balanced problem-finding and problem-solving
12. Positive/forward thinking
13. Energy and interest
14. Seeks new industry knowledge
15. Good conflict skills

Share and compare with team members. Then ask each person to choose just ONE to work on to increase their team skills.

Activity 4: Team Charter Sample Questions and Example

To improve members' openness to express their thoughts and to decrease *groupthink*, use a pre-session electronic survey. Then summarize the results for the group to process together in a session.

Sample Questions: (For the pre-session survey, select 6 – 10 or choose others important to the team)

1. What is the purpose that ties our work and hearts together?
2. What goals and priorities are most important right now?
3. How should we work together so we can do our best?
4. What should guide how we manage conflict?
5. What norms should shape how we meet?
6. What are the standards of quality we want for the team?
7. How do we hold ourselves accountable?
8. What does support for each other look like?
9. What should be our next level of thinking and working?
10. What legacy do we want to create?
11. What role does each person play on our team?

A sample of one team's charter is on the next page. Yours should meet your team's needs and address areas most important for your team.

Organization name Team Charter & Norms, DATE

Our shared purpose: *To ensure each child reaches his or her full potential and pave a path for each student's health, growth, and success in life.*

Who we are to each other: *We are collaborators and supporters.*

Our functions: *We work to achieve our strategic goals to have the impact we seek.*

How We Work Together, We…

- ☑ Leverage our culture of learning and celebrate our successes.
- ☑ We deliberately remove barriers and support the team's growth.
- ☑ Articulate a clear and shared vision that emotionally connects the team to our shared work.

To Ensure Effective Meetings, We…

- ☑ Begin and end meetings on time.
- ☑ Provide agendas in advance for input and follow them.
- ☑ Remain flexible for different work styles and cultural norms.
- ☑ Are fully present, giving each person our full attention.
- ☑ Record and revisit detailed minutes for our meetings.

To Ensure Emotional Safety, We…

- ☑ Create and seek opportunities to foster trust.
- ☑ Grant each other grace for intentions.
- ☑ Explore language that promotes greater inclusion.
- ☑ Cultivate spaces that embrace and include multiple perspectives.

For a Culture of Collaboration and Accountability, We…

- ☑ Center the needs of our constituents.
- ☑ Clearly define roles, responsibilities, and timelines.
- ☑ When there are issues of performance, come to each other directly and constructively first.
- ☑ Take responsibility when we make mistakes.
- ☑ Address concerns in the meeting and avoid "the meeting after the meeting."
- ☑ Execute on what we agreed upon.

Activity 5: Operationalizing Our Values

One consideration when working on team development is to reexamine the core values and decide how to improve alignment between those values and the team's behaviors. *Values are* important beliefs, principles, or ways of being that we hold. When they are "lived," we know them AND we shape and align our behaviors with them. The same is true at work. What are our organizational values and how do or should they shape our ways of working together to create the best work environment to accomplish our shared goals?

Team Reflection Activity

Our Values	**Actual behaviors that reflect this value**	***Non*-value centered behaviors that can impede our work**
Write each in this column *xxxxx*		

As you charter the team, have the team consider how to "live" the values. Explore: *What are the behaviors that demonstrate our values in our everyday work lives?*

Activity 6: Team interdependence: Sociogram Activity Kouzes and Posner[35]

This mapping helps team members realize they can do their jobs even better when they: 1) build better bonds; 2) are aware of others' intersections with their roles and 3) recognize others are valuable resources in achieving goals.

❶ First, have everyone introduce themselves, by saying their job role, how it contributes to the organization, key functions, special talents, and areas of passion. If it is a team smaller than eight or so, team members can ask questions for clarification.

❷ Team members should take notes on the graphic below so they can recall key information.

❸ Each person places their name in the center, then prints the name of each person on the team and their role. Then, for those whose roles are most critical to their immediate work, they darken the line.

❹ Team members share who (and how) their most critical connections should be, based on the darkened lines.

❺ Identify some simple next steps to connect with the key people and one other person who is important but not as critical to their job role to build synergies.

---

[35] Kouzes, J. and Posner, B., 2017. The Leadership Challenge Workbook.

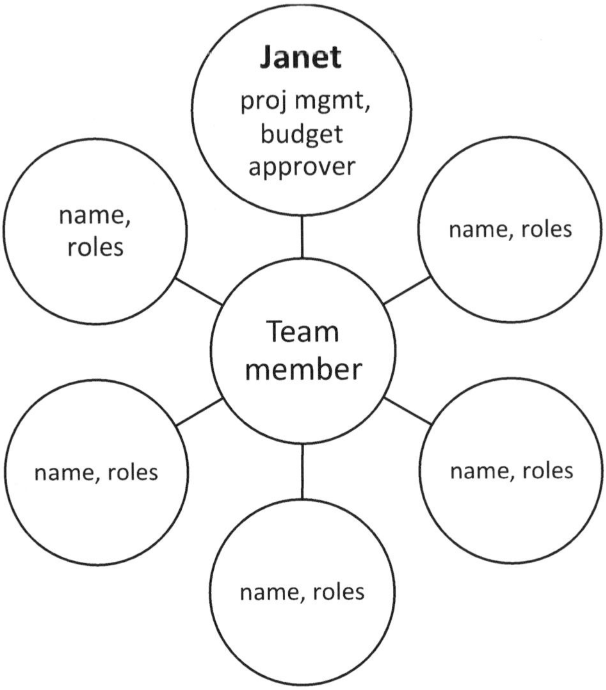

An alternate exercise

Use the diagram above (or just take notes), but this time, plan time to meet with 2-3 colleagues each month exchanging responses to some of these questions.

What is your job role? What are the most meaningful contributions you make to the organization in your role? What do you enjoy most about your work? What is causing you the most angst in your role at this time? What are the intersections with our work? What do you enjoy most outside of work?

Then, when the team is together, spend time introducing colleagues using this information. Continue, in subsequent months, until every team member has spent this individual time with all colleagues.

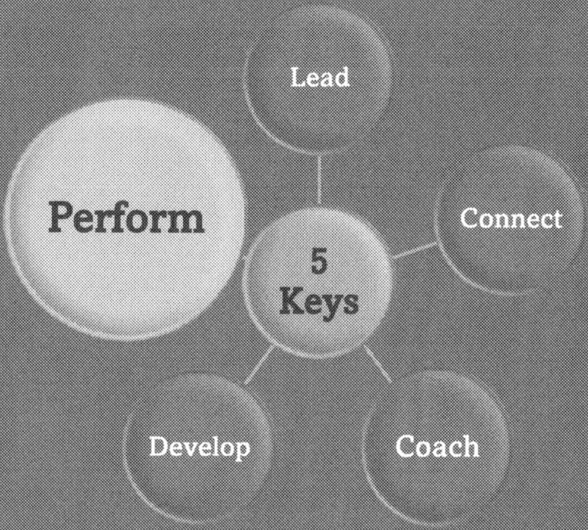

the PERFORM key

The "People Smart" Leader has a results-orientation and uses structures and practices that inspire people to perform their best work.

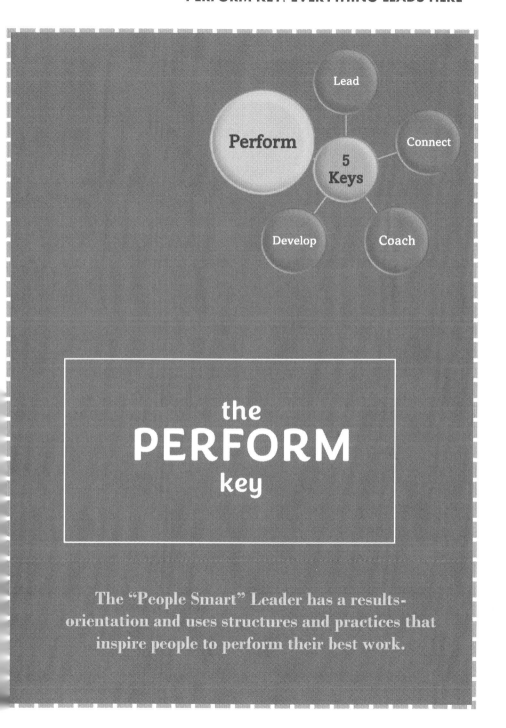

The Perform Key: All your efforts lead to performance.

Why are my team member's work outputs so uneven? Some give their all; others seem to just go through the motions. I get stressed doing performance appraisals with some of them; and sometimes I am not fully honest with appraisals because I don't want them to get upset.

Companies employ staff to achieve specific goals. Hiring is viewed as a sound investment of resources in pursuit of company goals that can positively affect customers and stakeholders.

An effective leader is keenly aware that their job is to lead people to achieve a set of results. As such, they put in place what is necessary for their people to consistently deliver their best work. For the People Smart Leader that means the other keys (addressed in Chapters 1-9)—LEAD, CONNECT, COACH, and DEVELOP—operate jointly, and are all directed towards one great aim—Performance.

Busy work is different from performance, so pay attention to setting goals, monitoring, supporting, adjusting goals, and appraising your team members' performance. The PERFORM KEY looks at what you can do to set up a culture of inspiration and high performance. That means putting in place factors and rhythms to realize and celebrate *valued* achievements.

If you have done most of what is covered in this book, your team's high performance can be both expected and inspiring. **Chapter 10** offers you some added insights.

Chapter 10

Performance: All Your Work Leads Here.

This chapter reminds you to keep your eye trained on the reason everyone has their job—to achieve valued RESULTS.

1. Embrace a results-orientation.
2. Elements to ensure your people are performance-ready.
3. Make accountability productive, painless, rhythmic.
4. A few thoughts about chronic under-performers.

Your job is to lead your people to achieve outstanding results on behalf of the organization. Your own evaluation measures the extent to which you and your direct reports evidence a high level of *actual* results. This book's entire aim is to support you in building a quality culture and processes that inspire your team to deliver stellar results.

Reflect: Think about *the People Smart Leader* keys addressed in chapters 1-9. They work together. Assume you are operationalizing one or two of this book's keys but not attending to the others. These examples underscore possible consequences of not activating all of the keys to evoke performance.

☑ What if you are actively building relationships (Connect) with your people only to say, *my people like me but they aren't doing their jobs?*

☑ What about a leader who is great setting direction, clarifying goals, and being courageous enough to implement major changes (aspects of the LEAD key) who ends up saying *my people have horrible attitudes, make excuses not to come to work, and lack motivation to try new methods of working?*

☑ Then take a leader who spends time with their people, listening and prompting them to reflect on their activities (COACH aspects), who ends up saying *my people appreciate our time, but they are all over the place with their goals.*

☑ Maybe you budget ample resources to allow your team to attend trainings, conferences, and shadow others (DEVELOP key elements), only to say *somehow all this training is not helping them to improve their work or apply it to their jobs.*

The point in those scenarios is that all of *these are inputs, drivers of performance,* that when **combined** evoke real accomplishment. One or two without the others will prove insufficient. The leader is cognizant of the difference between activity and performance; they plan staff activities, so they are clearly directed towards performance.

Remember, the goal is PERFORMANCE...Achievement...Results.

Lead + **Connect** + **Coach** + **Develop** ➔ **PERFORMANCE**

To perform means *to achieve or exceed value-adding required business results. These results are achieved in a way consistent with the organization's mission, values, and cultural standards.*

EMBRACE A RESULTS ORIENTATION

Effective leaders keep relentless attention on results. **To be results-oriented** means you are always mindful of outcomes and are committed to achieving them. It is true that some of the worst leaders are results-driven but act tyrannically in pursuit of these outcomes. They ride roughshod over people, their destructive patterns become clear to everyone, and many eventually derail as leaders. A skilled leader is also attuned to outcomes and puts in place practices, attitudes, and processes that *evoke and inspire* their people to perform their best.

Look again at the Zenger-Folkman graphic shared in Chapter 2 on page 64. It reinforces the connection between "people smarts" (i.e., relationship skills) and achieving results.

Reflection: What insights do you gain when exploring the connection between people skills and driving for results?

Exercise: Goal Clarity. One shortcoming for leaders in their effort to create a high-performance workplace is the use of ambiguous performance goals. This activity asks you to practice crafting clear, measurable goals for your staff team using the SMART or another framework. (SMART: Specific, Measurable, Achievable, Results, and Timebound).

Poorly or vaguely written	**Better written**
Improve customer service	Improve customer service scores from 70 to 75% by year end through training staff, incentives, and mentoring.
Improve written correspondence to stakeholders	Ensure all outgoing correspondence to stakeholders is edited and error free using new procedures and processes within three months.
Reduce # of job vacancies	Reduce turnaround for job fills to 45 days by year end by hiring two more recruiters, prioritizing, better manager relationships, and new sourcing strategies.
Offer positive feedback to staff more often	Increase positive feedback to direct reports by scheduling time weekly to write down what staffers did well and share with staffers in one-on-ones and send monthly "kudos" emails to team. Staff, in quarterly survey, report receiving more positive feedback.
Your example	
Your example	
Your example	

Crafting performance objectives, in partnership with the employee, takes time, practice and attention to become proficient. This is a worthy investment that creates clarity and agreement on what actual performance is, removing confusion for everyone.

ELEMENTS TO ENSURE PEOPLE ARE PERFORMANCE-READY

Stop! Before you begin making judgements about your team members, ask yourself: *What aspects of my style and methods have the most direct influence on my staffers performing their best?*

Exercise: Here are some questions to ask yourself related to the PERFORM key. Place a check (✓) on those you already do. Circle those that are your areas of opportunity. These reinforce and are slightly different than questions posed in Chapter 3 (page 86).

1. Do I set goals in *partnership* with my direct reports (which encourages their commitment)?
2. Do I hold the belief that I have a vital role in creating an environment that *inspires* people to perform rather than using badgering to get them to perform?
3. Are the *goals clear*, achievable, and measurable so there is little chance of confusion between me and each report?
4. Do I ensure the team members have the *resources* they need to do their work successfully, such as space, materials, coaching and feedback, support people, skill-building, etc.?
5. Am I competent at balancing *empathy* with the expectation of performance *accountability*?

6. Am I *flexible appraising performance* when environmental factors create barriers to achieving expected performance?

7. Am I *fair and unbiased* in appraising all direct reports?

8. Do I act courageously and decisively when *addressing chronic low performance*?

9. Do I provide *rewards and incentives* for achieving desired performance year-round and annually?

10. Do I have a *rhythm of check-ins* with direct reports about their progress, status, support needs, and challenges related to achieving their goals?

11. Do I prepare myself to have quality, *honest conversations* about less-than-needed performance that offer staffers a chance to improve before year-end evaluations?

12. Do I ensure there are action items (and due dates) at the end of *meetings* and check on those actions during the next one?

13. Do I encourage my staff to *give me feedback* about my projects to foster a culture of holding each other accountable?

One area (from items 1-13 above) that I will pay more attention to: ______________________________________, and this is how I will do so ______________________________________

Review the graphic on the next page which uses six items to summarize the key work environment factors addressed by the 13 questions above. They *enhance* people's performance when they are present or *inhibit* them from doing their best work when absent. Your job is to fine-tune the factors needed for your direct reports to be inspired and **ready to perform**. Look at the six areas. **Mark any of the six where you need to do a bit more work.**

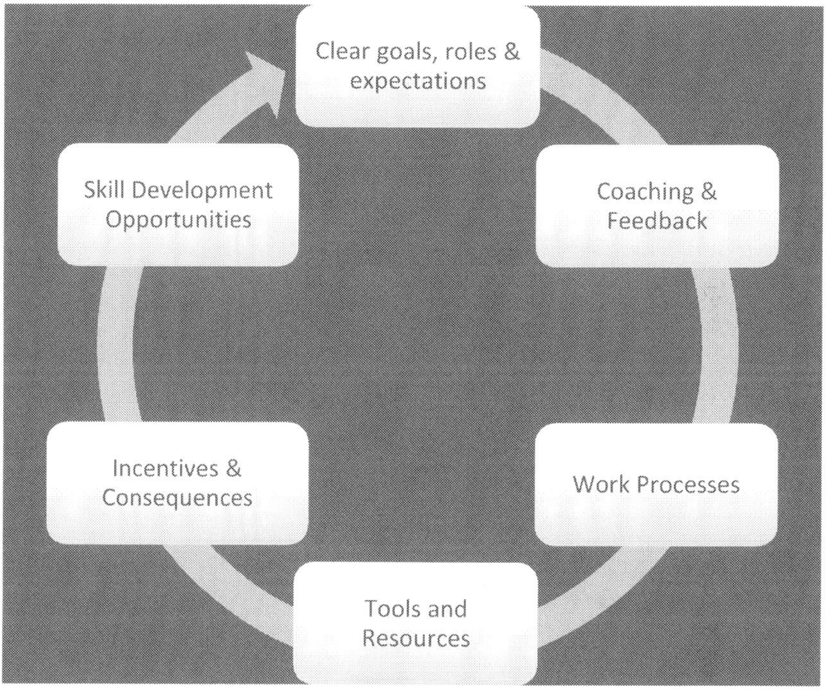

MAKE ACCOUNTABILITY PRODUCTIVE, PAINLESS, RHYTHMIC

People often think of accountability in a negative light, but it is a powerful way to foster work positivity. Think of accountability in this light, and you are on your way to stronger team performance.

Accountability is defined as: *how people take ownership of their commitments, to hold people to account, or to be responsible for their actions.*

The power of accountability lies in how it:

- Is an indicator that what people are doing is important.
- Helps team members stay focused on the right things, when competing tasks can deplete their time.
- Encourages people to do their work with efficiency and focus.
- Helps give people a feeling of accomplishment related to specific goals.
- Supports increased staff dedication and morale, which leads to improved performance.
- Is a way to demonstrate fairness across the work team.
- Helps build trust, cooperation, and responsibility in the team.

The cost of no or low accountability: A work culture lacking accountability leads to frustration, unfulfilled tasks, lower morale, an atmosphere of confused priorities, and it negatively impacts others' work across the team.

Make performance accountability rhythmic. This is fairly straight forward. Your accountability processes should be predictable, planned, and purposeful. That means setting up a schedule of performance goal check-ins throughout the year, not just at year-end. Additionally, in your one-on-one meetings, you ought to include progress checks as needed; these are different from more formal performance goal checkpoints.

These scheduled checkpoints should be structured. You can use a set of simple questions like the ones below on a quarterly (or other) basis:

1. Please walk through your performance objectives for the year and give an update on where you are on each one so far.
2. How do you feel about your progress?
3. What will it take for you to achieve your objectives?
4. Is there anything getting in the way of your success?
5. What support do you need from me (or others) to achieve your goals by year-end?
6. If you were to predict how well you will achieve your goals by year end, what would you say?

Another option: Have the staffer come to the planned checkpoint with 1) their responses (to questions 1-6 above) related to each of their goals, and 2) a plan of action to achieve their best on the goals.

What makes accountability virtually painless? There is a small chance of painful official performance reviews when you have all the items under *"Elements to Ensure People are Performance Ready"* (pages 231-233) in place. You will have established an environment where people know what's expected; receive what they need to do their jobs; have regular, supportive conversations about successes and shortfalls; and they are accustomed to a positive accountability culture that challenges and motivates them.

Celebrate, don't punish high performance through neglect. Not only can accountability be painless, but leaders should also acknowledge and encourage high performance. They use a range of incentives and celebrations, from raises, promotions, public acknowledgements, praise, confirming feedback, special assignments, and more.

Spend time looking forward: The official performance appraisal meeting, when there is a rhythm of checkpoints year-round, can be spent being developmental, i.e., looking forward. Since the previous year's performance ratings should be fairly clear (even predictable), after confirming the evaluation of the previous year, use the formal appraisal meeting time to set the stage to establish conditions for even better performance. Use such questions as:

- How would you describe where the organization is going?
- What are the opportunities in your role to make an even bigger contribution to the organization's goals next year?
- What specific areas of our work would you like to dedicate more of your time and talents to?
- In your job role, where do you see the chances for improving our processes, our products, or anything else?
- How do you see yourself growing as a professional next year?

Make a note: What can you do to make accountability productive and painless? ____

____

ABOUT CHRONIC UNDER-PERFORMERS

When their best work is not good enough. Even when you do all you know to do to adopt better leadership practices, there are a few times when staffers perform below expectations. Avoiding chronic low performance is not a sound strategy.

Before making major changes to a staffers' personnel status, be sure you have done a reasonably good job in setting conditions for them to do well. In some cases where historically high performers become lower performers, what might remedy the situation is to try to uncover: WHY has the change occurred? Then WHAT do they need to get back on track? In other cases, *is this person someone, since their hire, who has never met the needed standards?* In another instance, the question may be: *Has the job evolved beyond what appears to be their capacity, or can they upskill to keep pace?* (If the latter is the case, move quickly to provide the development needed for the staffer.) Neither of these scenarios means you should erode the culture of high performance by settling for low performance.

If nothing evokes the needed changes in performance (connecting, coaching, developing, accountability measures, and more), hopefully the low-performing staffer has realized it, and they make the choice to find a better fit. If not, seek assistance to develop a humane approach when you must transition them out.

Work with your human resources specialist to determine how to do the best job of exiting people in a respectful way that offers them a chance to fill the gap between job loss and new job acquisition.

This closes Chapter 10, the Perform Key chapter. Try this final PERFORM KEY activity before moving on.

Exercise: 90-Day Plan to Upgrade Team Performance

Use the chart below to think about then identify things you will do to sustain, improve, or increase your direct reports' high performance.

Action	Time period	Expected Results
Ex. Share vision more often so staffers sense more meaning to their work		
Ex. Do regular checkpoints so people know where they stand and can adjust what they do		

This closes all ten chapters of *The People Smart Leader* book. Take a break and reflect on how you have or will elevate your effectiveness in leading your people to outstanding accomplishments.

Then take time to flip back through the chapters, your notes, or the Table of Contents to capture your Key Takeaways on the next page.

Closing *The People Smart Leader* Book

You have made it through *The People Smart Leader* book, exploring the Five Keys to Inspire People to do their best work. Surely, there have been some concepts, ideas, and action steps you can add to your "People Leader" skill repertoire. So, rather than trying to think of all of them, take time to note your Key Takeaways here.

My Key Takeaways

Changes I am prioritizing: If I had to choose no more than five specific ways to change my approach over the next six to twelve months to enhance my people leadership skills, I choose these five:

1.
2.
3.
4.
5.

Consider yearly revisiting the book, then target specific areas. Never bite off too much, since even one change is known to have positive ripple effects. **Thanks for your leadership. It matters.**

Acknowledgements

I extend gratitude to the special communities throughout my adult years that provided the experiences, support, challenge, and inspiration for me to lead and help others do the same. I thank those who, in my early years, just believed I could lead, those who somehow grew because I was there, and those who functioned as experiment participants while I developed the skills, demeanor and commitment to become an effective leader.

Specifically, I acknowledge the Pan African Orthodox Christian Church community during those neophyte years. With you, I learned about group dynamics, human relationships, and leadership while embracing a philosophy that real leaders are humanistic and skilled at helping to unlock the vast, mostly unrealized potential of people.

During my next two decades as a nonprofit leader, I am gratified I was afforded the autonomy to lead, learn, innovate, structure, think, restructure, hire, release, then segue into hiring better, developing, coaching, engaging, and empowering people to achieve at elevated levels. For that, I thank the Detroit YMCA and YMCA of the USA.

I am also indebted to my coaching and consulting partner-clients. These pages emerged because you trusted me with your goals, inner lives, thoughts, and fascinating stories. Collaborating with you has been confirmative of my espoused belief that people really can keep growing, regardless of age or experience.

There is no denying the immeasurable value of the support I received from my partners for life. My husband, Sondai, has been there as a thinking companion, lifting out stories that I had passed over, and our daughter Noni, herself a people and talent executive and my partner in the people work. I adore you for the courage to test, refine, offer feedback, and contemporize my words and ideas.

I am grateful to the people who gifted me their time and attention to do a pre-publication review of *The People Smart Leader*. They include Uwimana Olabisi, John Stoyka, Krystle Starvis, Destini Hylton, Jerrie Witherspoon, Darrin Anderson PhD, Monishae O'Neill, Anita Stovall, and Vanessa Stovall. Your impressions, insights, corrections, and comments were immensely helpful. Finally, I acknowledge my friends Cynthia Ward PhD, Jackie Gordon, and Diane Jackson PhD. You are always available to hear me and help me make meaning of my experiences, and you have contributed some of your own to what's contained in this publication.

Author Profile

Lindiwe Stovall Lester spent 40 years doing *the people work* described in *The Everyday Leader* and here in *The People Smart Leader*. She is partner with top and mid-level leaders--coaching and mentoring as they increase their mastery leading and inspiring others for high achievement. Currently, as the founder and president of Tap In Consulting, she limits her work of transformation to executive coaching, team realignment and development, and consulting around key human performance factors.

She retired as a national nonprofit senior leader, partnered with chief executives and their boards of directors. Her body of work centered on executive development, new executive transition, strategic thinking and planning, raising the level of board effectiveness, and enhancing the competencies of colleagues in consulting roles.

A lifelong learner, Lindiwe makes sure she includes people from multiple generations in her circle to both enliven her understanding and stay abreast of changes and trends. A committed advocate for access and inclusion, Ms. Lester remains involved in coaching and mentoring current and emerging leaders-of-color.

Lindiwe holds master's and post-master's degrees in instructional and human performance systems. She is certified in executive coaching, performance consulting, social and emotional intelligence coaching, behavior analytics, and executive presence coaching.

Her family and friends, writing, art, and travel assume big spaces in her re-fired retirement life.

Index

Made in the USA
Columbia, SC
02 November 2024

45273604R10135